ookstand Bookwork Bookends Bookrack Bookwork Bookman Booklist Bookstall Bookreader Book

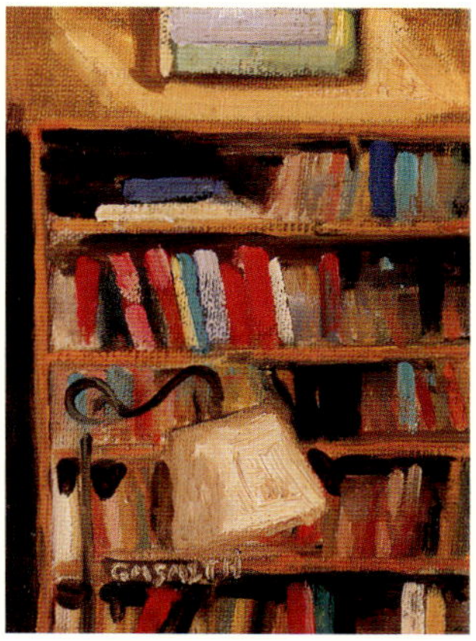

This edition of

The Art of the Bookstore

is published to commemorate the

40th Anniversary of

Gibbs Smith, Publisher.

Gibbs M. Smith

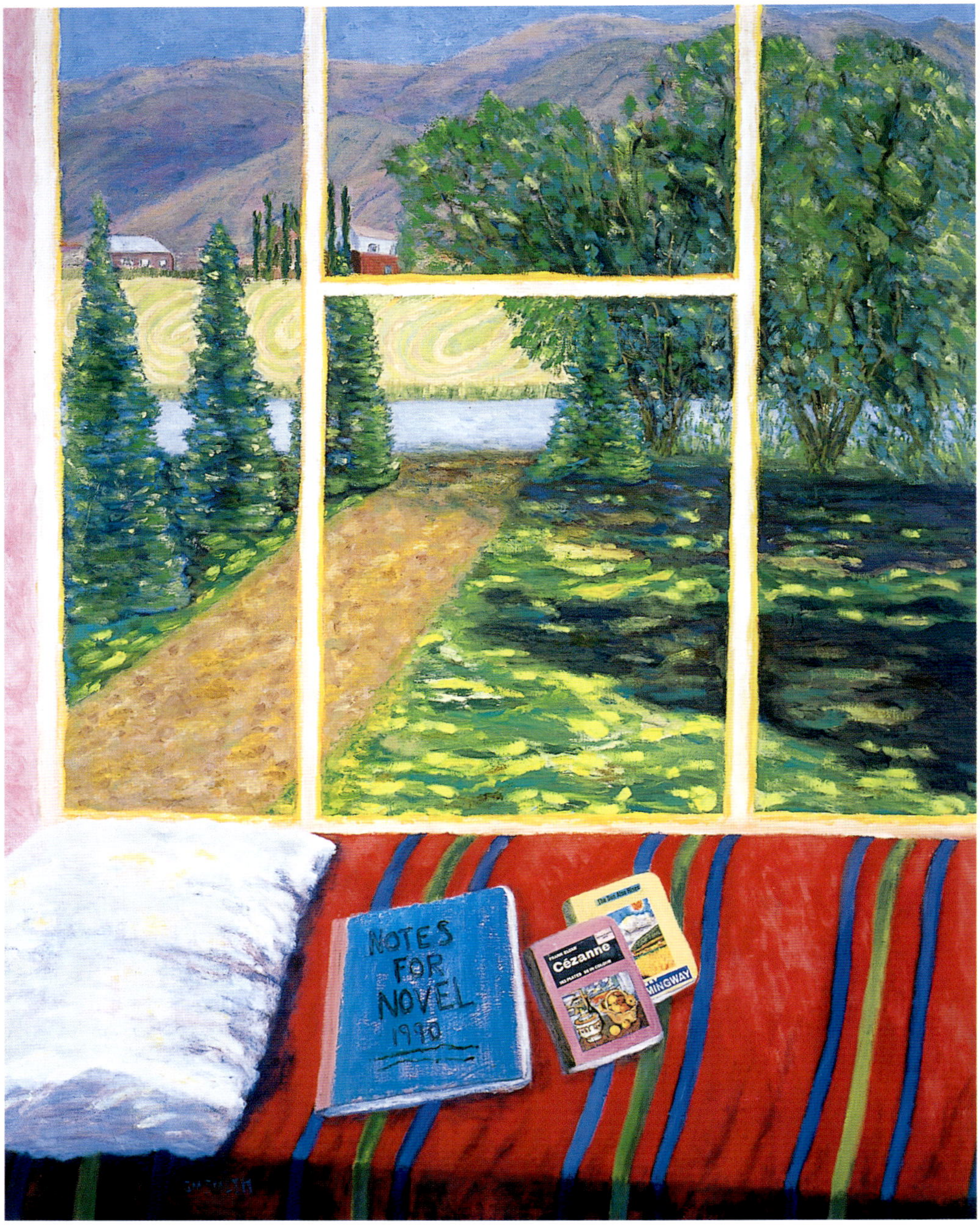

Gibbs M. Smith, View from My Window, *1984. Oil on linen, 16" × 20".*

The ART of the BOOKSTORE

THE BOOKSTORE PAINTINGS OF GIBBS M. SMITH

GIBBS SMITH
TO ENRICH AND INSPIRE HUMANKIND
Salt Lake City | Charleston | Santa Fe | Santa Barbara

First Edition
13 12 11 10 09 5 4 3 2 1

Published by
Gibbs Smith, Publisher
P.O. Box 667
Layton, Utah 84041

1.800.835.4993 orders
www.gibbs-smith.com

Interiors designed by Steve Jerman
Printed and bound in China
Gibbs Smith books are printed on either recycled, 100% post-consumer waste, FSC-certified papers or on paper produced from a 100% certified sustainable forest/controlled wood source.

Library of Congress Cataloging-in-Publication Data

Smith, Gibbs M.
The art of the bookstore : the bookstore paintings of Gibbs M. Smith / Gibbs M. Smith. — 1st ed.
p. cm.
ISBN-13: 978-1-4236-0643-7
ISBN-10: 1-4236-0643-4
1. Smith, Gibbs M. 2. Bookstores in art. I. Title.
ND237.S596A4 2009
381'.450020973—dc22
2009013679

When I get a little money, I buy books; and if any is left, I buy food and clothes.

—Desiderius Erasmus

In developing my own practice as a painter I appreciate the friendship and association of several people who are wonderful artists and who have shared their knowledge with me: Earl Jones, Randall Lake, Dennis Phillips, Alexandra Blantyre, John Erickson, and photographer Michael Jenkins.

Thank you to all the members of the book community who contributed to this book: Roger Moss, Richard Abel, Steve Riggio, Anne Kubek, Barbara Siepker, Davis Dutton, Edward Borins, Kevin Ryan, Ken Sanders, Clark Kepler, Betsy Burton, Michael Powell, Gayle Shanks, Kerry Slattery, George and Sally Kiskaddon, Dee and Chuck Robinson, and Midge Dey. Thanks also to my editor, Lisa Anderson, and my assistant, Anita Wood.

Contents

It was clear that the books owned the shop rather than the other way about. Everywhere they had run wild and taken possession of their habitat, breeding and multiplying and clearly lacking any strong hand to keep them down.

—Agatha Christie, *The Clocks*

All good books are alike in that they are truer than if they had really happened and after you are finished reading one you will feel that all that happened to you and afterwards it all belongs to you; the good and the bad, the ecstasy, the remorse, and sorrow, the people and the places and how the weather was.

—Ernest Hemingway

Introduction

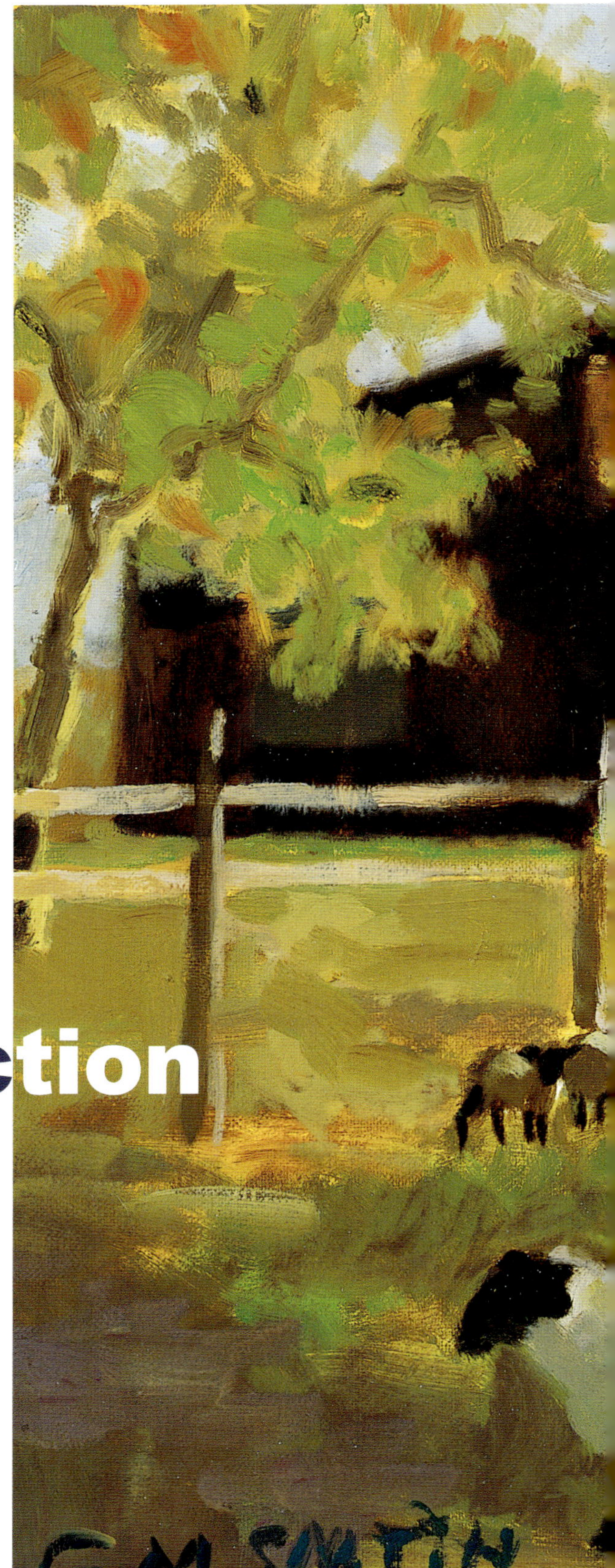

Gibbs M. Smith, Our Barn Office, *1989.*
Oil on linen, 16" × 20".

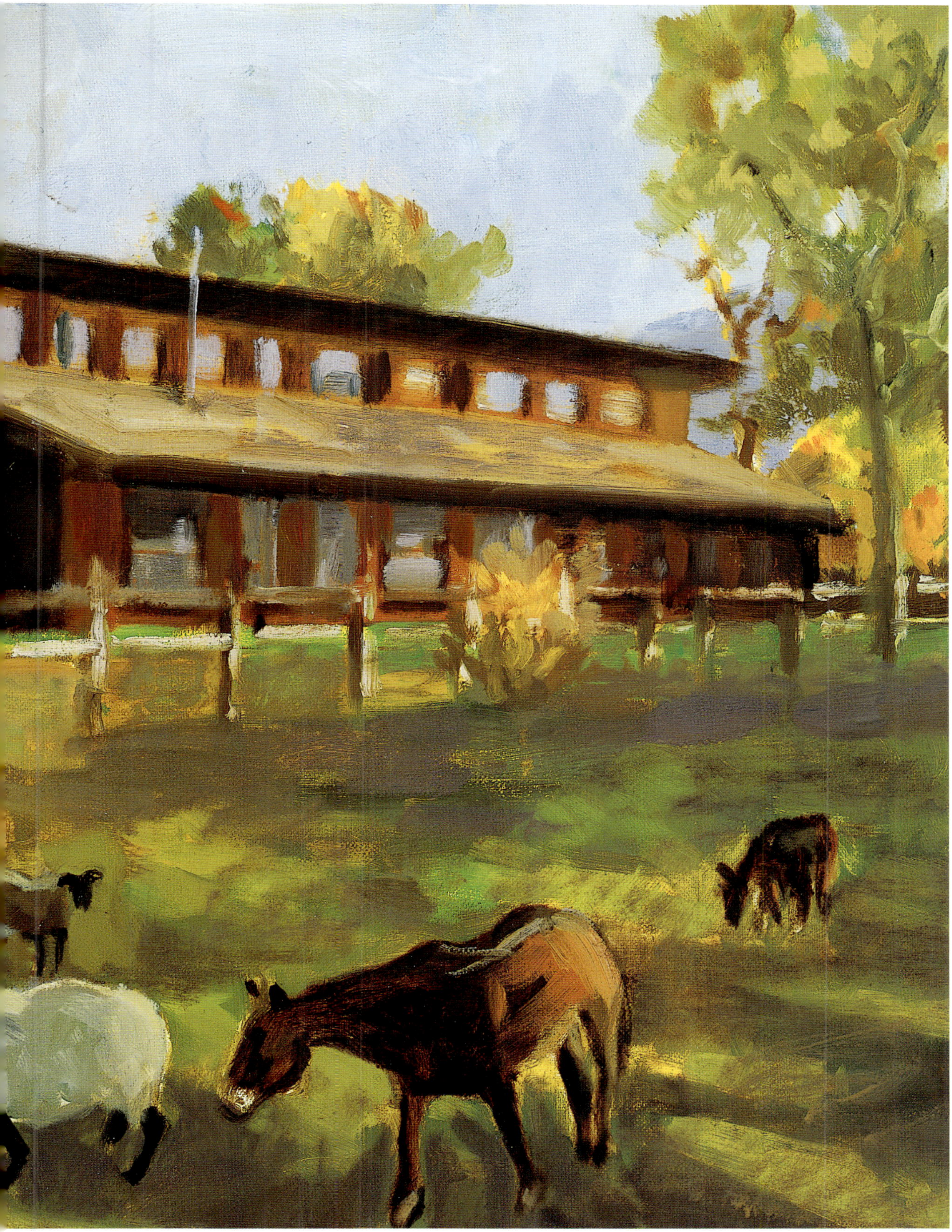

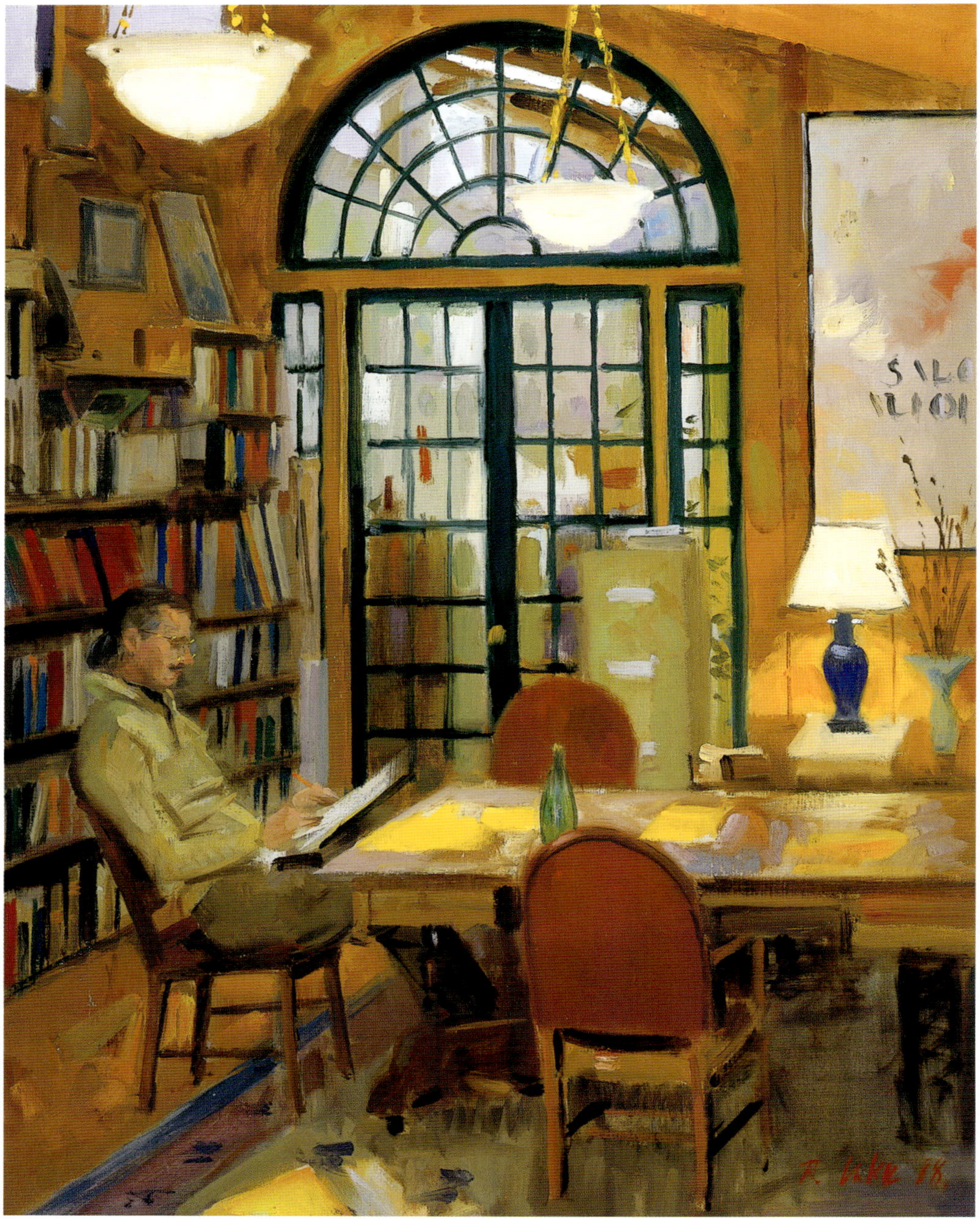

Randall Lake, Painting of Gibbs in His Office, *1991. Oil on canvas, 16" × 20".*

Ever since I was a child, I have felt that books are more than just the sum of their parts. Books are the physical embodiment of ideas, which are ephemeral. When the elements of a book come together, magic sometimes happens. It follows, then, that bookstores too are more than just bricks and mortar, shelves and hardcovers and paperbacks. When you combine so many books—so many voices, opinions, stories, and ideas—into one space, a creative and cultural fire often ignites.

For forty years, I have been extremely fortunate to participate actively in the book industry as a publisher. But my love of books, bookstores, and the people in the industry goes back much further, to my earliest memories.

During my years as a child in Oakland, Berkeley, and San Francisco, California, in the early 1940s, my mother would take me on walks, where she opened my eyes to the world. She would rub my hand over a stone that had been lying in the sun to feel the heat, or put it against the rough-smooth bark of a tree. Often we would go into her favorite stores, one of which was Gumps in San Francisco, for whom she designed windows. We would also visit John Howell Books. There she would help me buy books of my own. From these earliest memories two things were impressed upon me and have become part of my life—appreciation for nature and the natural world, and a love of books.

When I was about ten years old, my family moved to Utah and I gradually became aware of my own preferences and interests apart from my parents', such as which writers I personally liked, some of whom were Ernest Hemingway and Jack London. My father, a dentist who also loved literature, took me to Salt Lake City to Sam Weller's Book Store and purchased for me copies of *For Whom the Bell Tolls* and *The Sun Also Rises,* along with a collection of Jack London stories. I remember this very clearly, especially how Sam Weller himself took a personal interest in me as a young customer and helped me find the right books.

I came to realize as an adult what an enormous gift it was to have my own shelf, my own library, my favorite books that were my companions and that I read over and over. I firmly believe today as an adult that for the book world to be nourished and to survive, there needs to be a continual group of new book lovers nurtured by their parents.

I was very encouraged last fall when I was fortunate enough to lead a panel at a publishing conference. The panel was made up of young people from Portland, Oregon, area high schools and colleges, and we talked about the importance or lack of importance of books in their lives. Virtually all of the students spoke passionately about the value of the traditional book. They're familiar with all the electronic media and use it, but when they want to read a book, they want the real thing. Many of the students mentioned the same experience that I had—that their love of books came from their parents taking them to bookstores and buying them books of their own. From the earliest years, bookstores were part of their lives.

In the February 24, 2009, issue of *Bookselling This Week*, a memorial to John Updike stated that Updike thought of bookstores as "citadels of light." He spoke of his college days at Harvard, where he "marveled at the wealth of bookstores around Harvard Square." He commented on the transforming effect of technology on books and libraries and expressed concern over the possible loss of the physical book. He made a plea to those invested in the fate of the paper-and-ink book by saying, "Books traditionally have edges: some are rough-cut, some are smooth-cut, and a few, at least at my extravagant publishing house, are even top-stained. In the electronic anthill, where are the edges? The book revolution, which, from the Renaissance on, taught men and women to cherish and cultivate their individuality, threatens to end in a sparkling cloud of snippets."

Updike continued, "So, booksellers, defend your lonely forts. Keep your edges dry. Your edges are our edges. For some of us, books are intrinsic to our sense of personal identity."

Bookstores can have such an impact beyond enlightening and informing the customer through the books they buy there. Over the years I have seen many stores become community gathering places, locations of intellectual stimulation and education.

At Sam Weller's, I made a lifelong friend in both Sam and the store. Through my college years at the University of Utah I would frequently visit Sam's store and have many discussions with him about the book world. He was on the board of the American Bookseller's Association and knew many in the business. I liked

> The walls of books around him, dense with the past, formed a kind of insulation against the present world and its disasters.
>
> **—Ross MacDonald**

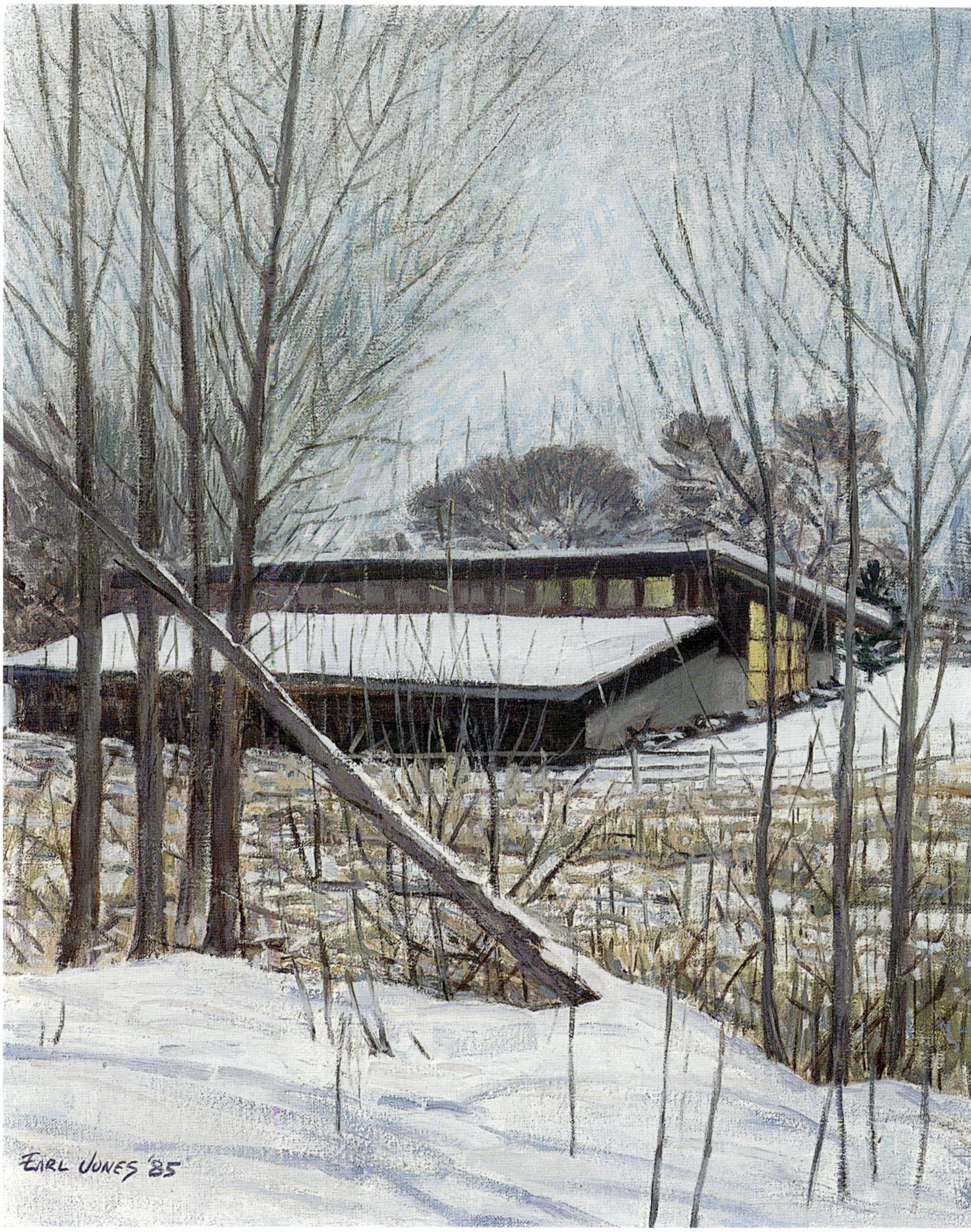

Earl Jones, Barn Office in the Winter, *1985. Oil on canvas.*

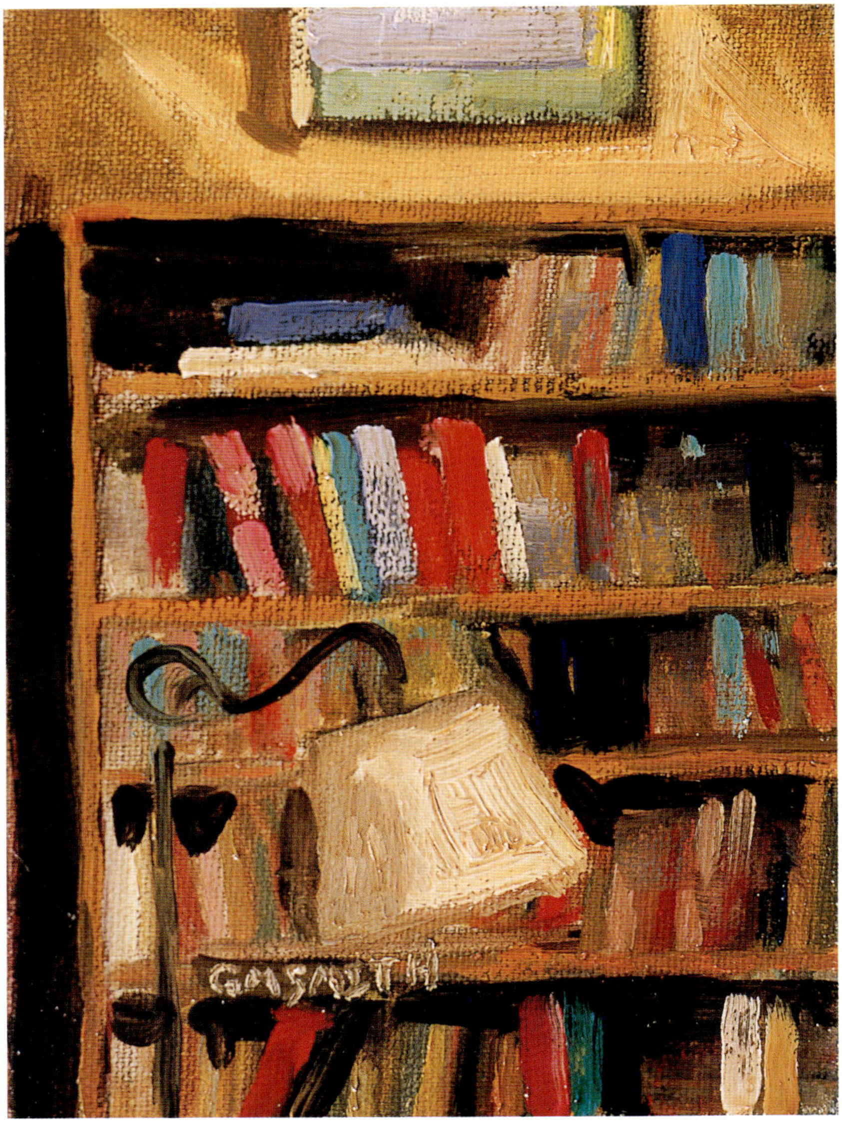

Gibbs M. Smith, My Bookshelf, *1985. Oil on canvas.*

to ask him about publishers, and he said that over the years most publishers had come into his store and visited, some on a regular basis. Alfred Knopf would come fairly often. Bennett Cerf had been there, and many more. I began to get the feeling that the book business was a community of people who knew each other and whose main goal in life was to create and sell books. This way of life appealed to me. Over the years, I've reflected on the nature of this industry, and I think it truly was, and to some degree still is, a cottage industry. It's unlike any other business.

The first store that I painted was City Lights in San Francisco, owned by Lawrence Ferlinghetti. In my twenties I had become fascinated with the beat generation—Jack Kerouac, Allen Ginsberg, Lawrence Ferlinghetti, and Gary Snyder. As a college freshman, I would drive with friends from Salt Lake City to San Francisco and hang out at North Beach to see the beat poets—and to go to City Lights, which I felt was the mecca of the book world at that time. Those walls, those people, and the books I bought there remain part of me, and Lawrence Ferlinghetti has remained a very good friend. I greatly admire him as a bookseller, poet, artist, and writer. The first exhibit of my paintings was held in his store, City Lights. This store remains important in my life.

In college I also found myself exploring all kinds of bookstores. My passion in college was to study Joe Hill, the IWW radical, laborer, and martyr, and this passion led me to write and publish a book that has become a standard on Hill. Doing my research, I haunted many bookstores around the country that focused on labor and liberal politics. It dawned on me that each bookstore I visited had its own personality; each store reflected the owner's personal passions and tastes. This variety of personalities, passions, and interests makes up an important part of the cultural fabric of our world. Bookstores are like universities, a place where your mind expands, your interests broaden, and your tastes evolve.

What gives a bookstore a personality? Is it the books organized on the shelves? Is it the character of the building that houses the bookstore? Is it the owner? Is it the staff? I can't answer the question I pose. All I can say is I can feel a personality in each store that I visit. It's more than an individual. It's more than the physical location. It's almost magical. The store develops a personality. The store itself becomes an old friend. You're glad it's there, glad you can visit, glad that you can have the connection through the varying phases of your own life. That's why it's very sad when a great store ceases operation—it's like the loss of an old friend. There's an emotional connection. It hurts when a store closes.

Reflections on the Book Trade

BY ROGER MOSS

I was an independent publishers' rep for thirty-five years, and let me say that it was one of the coolest jobs in the book trade. One of the best aspects of the job was the people I worked with. At both the publisher and the bookstore level, the folks were knowledgeable, smart, honest, and dedicated and excited about their work and its cultural significance. They were also often idiosyncratic, opinionated, autodidactic, and eccentric. They were complicated men and women, and they were a huge amount of fun to be around.

Every day of my job was an education. I learned not only about the book business but also about diverse subjects, from aa (rough, scoriaceous lava, a useful word for Scrabble players) to zyzzogeton (a genus of large South American leaf hoppers). Another great part of my job was knowing that in my own small way I was making a difference in the world of letters.

As I grew older, it was a satisfaction to help younger publishers and booksellers find their way in a complicated business and to learn from them the new technologies that they were introducing into the business, especially in accounting and inventory control.

The job of selling books, however, in the end always falls to people, not technology. The connection between author and her reader may filter through the publisher, the editor, the rep, the bookstore buyer, and the clerk on the sales floor, but the circle is completed when the reader settles down in a soft chair under a good light and begins to share the author's world.

The relationship between a bookstore and its patron is more than commerce, more than business; it's an emotional and spiritual connection.

One of the reasons I like painting bookstores, besides trying to honor the bookstore in my own way, is to try to capture the store's personality. This ephemeral quality, this aura, is what I try to capture with paint.

• • • • •

My interest in painting began when I was a child. My mother was a passionate artist and she introduced me to the joy of painting in oil. I came to love the smell of oil paint and turpentine, the sensual delight of putting paint on canvas. So I've always painted—first as a child with her; but then my own taste evolved through the study of art history and the painters who inspired me—John Sloan, Edward Hopper, Pierre Bonnard, and others. I've come to realize that I see the world not only through my own eyes but also through the eyes of artists that I love.

It was from books that I learned to see the world from the eyes of a painter and poet. When I walk down a rainy city street,

I think of Walt Whitman or Pierre Bonnard (who spoke of crude seeing and intelligent seeing—his ideas opened my eyes); also the artist Albert Marquet (I love his casual gestures with a brush); or Edward Hopper (and his love of the commonplace); all of whom I first met through books. I read about them in books long before I went to galleries and museums and saw their work. I could see what they saw and what makes a soggy evening in the city—with streetlights and store lights reflecting on wet pavement—so appealing. My favorite thing is to be in a city, in the rain, and to go to a bookstore and see the shining lights of the store, the people congregating in the store, the bright colors of the books shining through the wet evening. So many of my paintings have that feeling. My experiences in New York City have been important in my life as a painter, both from exploring the city's museums and paintings and from the city itself, which taught me a lot about what I respond to as a painter. New York is one of my favorite subjects to paint, especially in the evening in the rain.

I am extremely fortunate to have spent forty years working with books and the people whose lives are centered around them—writers, publishers, booksellers, agents, bookstore owners and employees, and, of course, the individual citizens of the world who nourish this industry by buying books. Those readers and the people who feel passionately about books are the true heroes of the book community. Most people who work in this industry would not trade it for any other career, even if it would pay considerably more. It's a way of life to be in the book world.

Our mission statement at Gibbs Smith, Publisher, is "To Enrich and Inspire Humankind," and my favorite quote by Walt Whitman states: "My spirit has pass'd in compassion and determination around the whole earth, I have look'd for equals and lovers and found them ready for me in all lands." For many years I have kept these ideals in mind as I helped chart our company's course.

My hope is that we at Gibbs Smith, Publisher, and everyone in the book industry can continue to make magic happen through books.

I have always imagined that Paradise will be a kind of library.

—Jorge Luis Borges

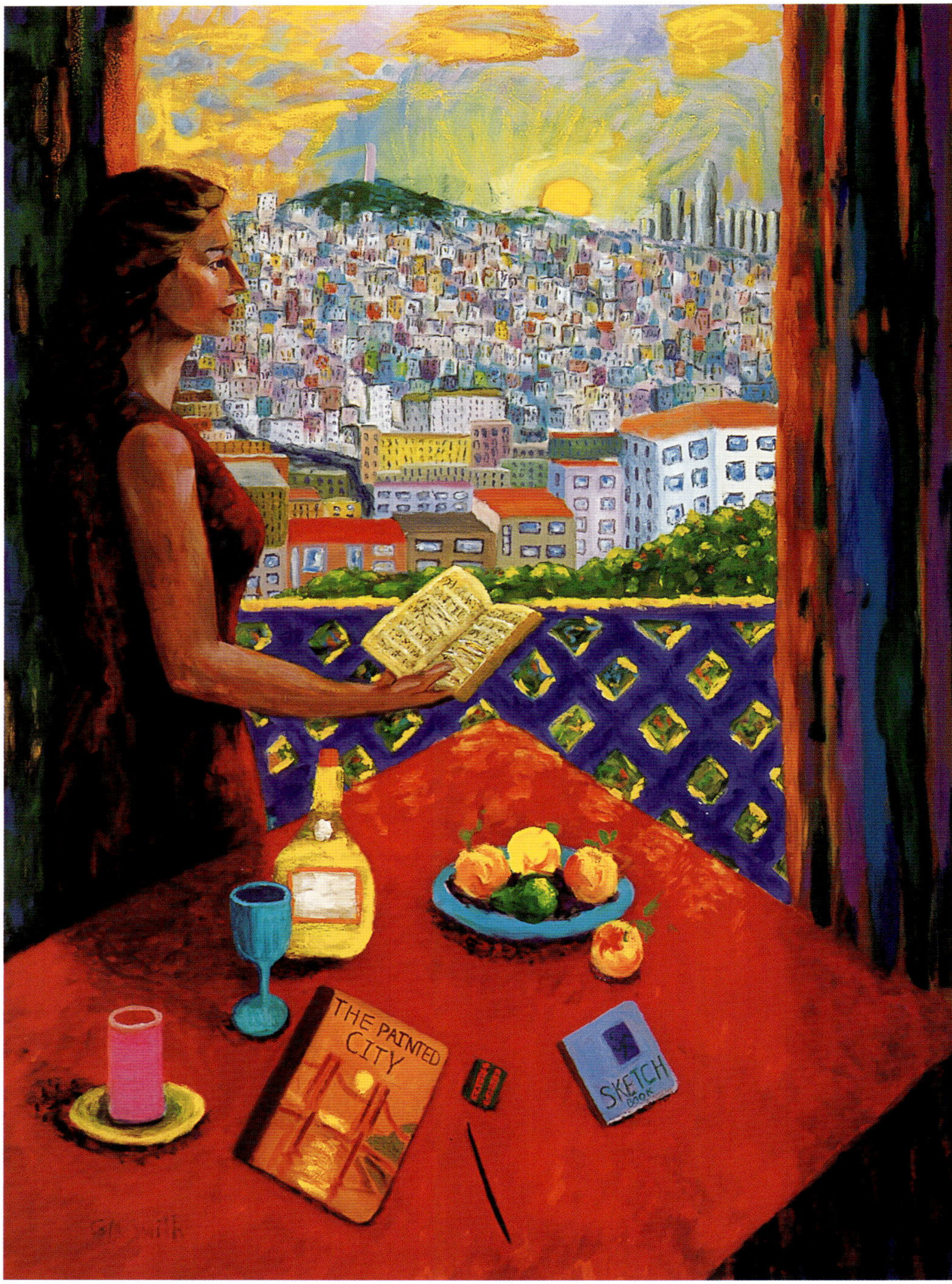

Gibbs M. Smith, San Francisco Afternoon, *1983. Oil on canvas, 16" × 20".*

Leaving any bookstore is hard, especially on a day in August, when the street outside burns and glares, and the books inside are cool and crisp to the touch; especially on a day in January, when the wind is blowing, the ice is treacherous, and the books inside seem to gather together in colorful warmth. It's hard to leave a bookstore any day of the year, though, because a bookstore is one of the few places where all the cantankerous, conflicting, alluring voices of the world co-exist in peace and order, and the avid reader is as free as a person can possibly be, because she is free to choose among them.

—Jane Smiley

To sit alone in the lamplight with a book spread out before you, and hold intimate converse with men of unseen generations—such is a pleasure beyond compare.

—Yosida Kenko

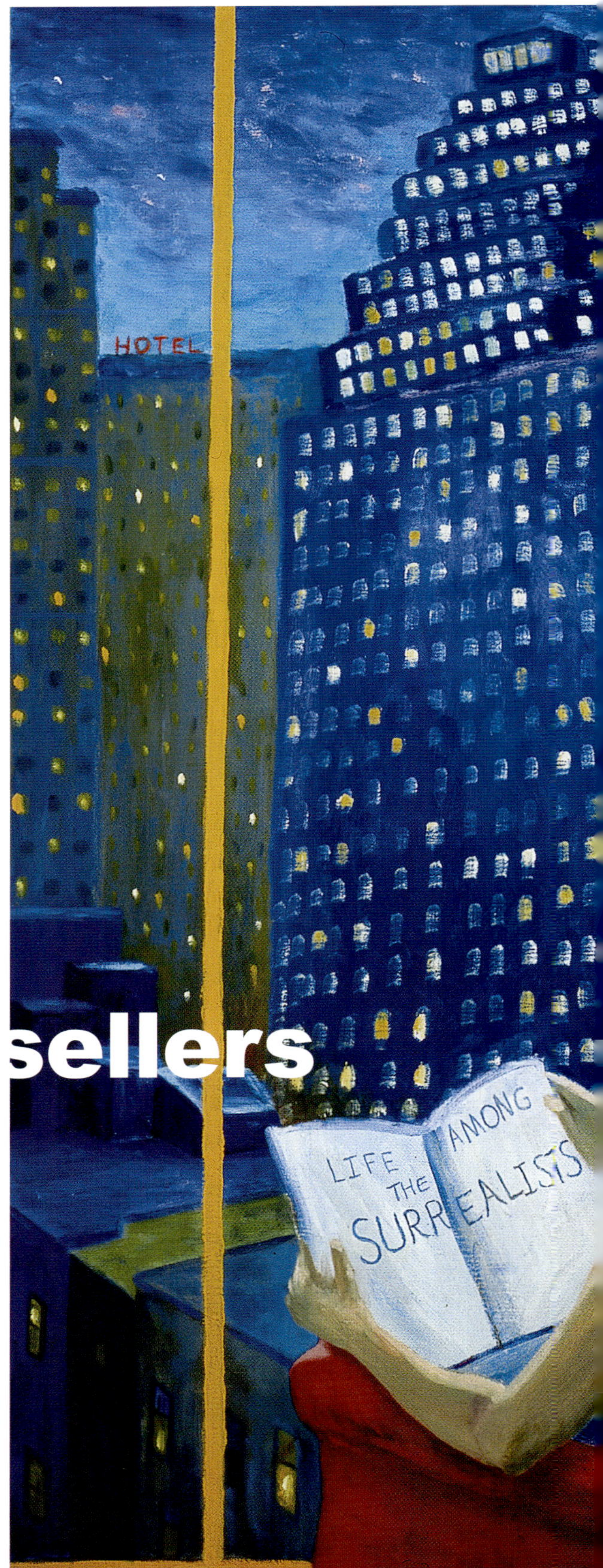

Booksellers

Gibbs M. Smith, Life among the Surrealists, Manhattan, *1990. Oil on canvas, 30" × 40".*

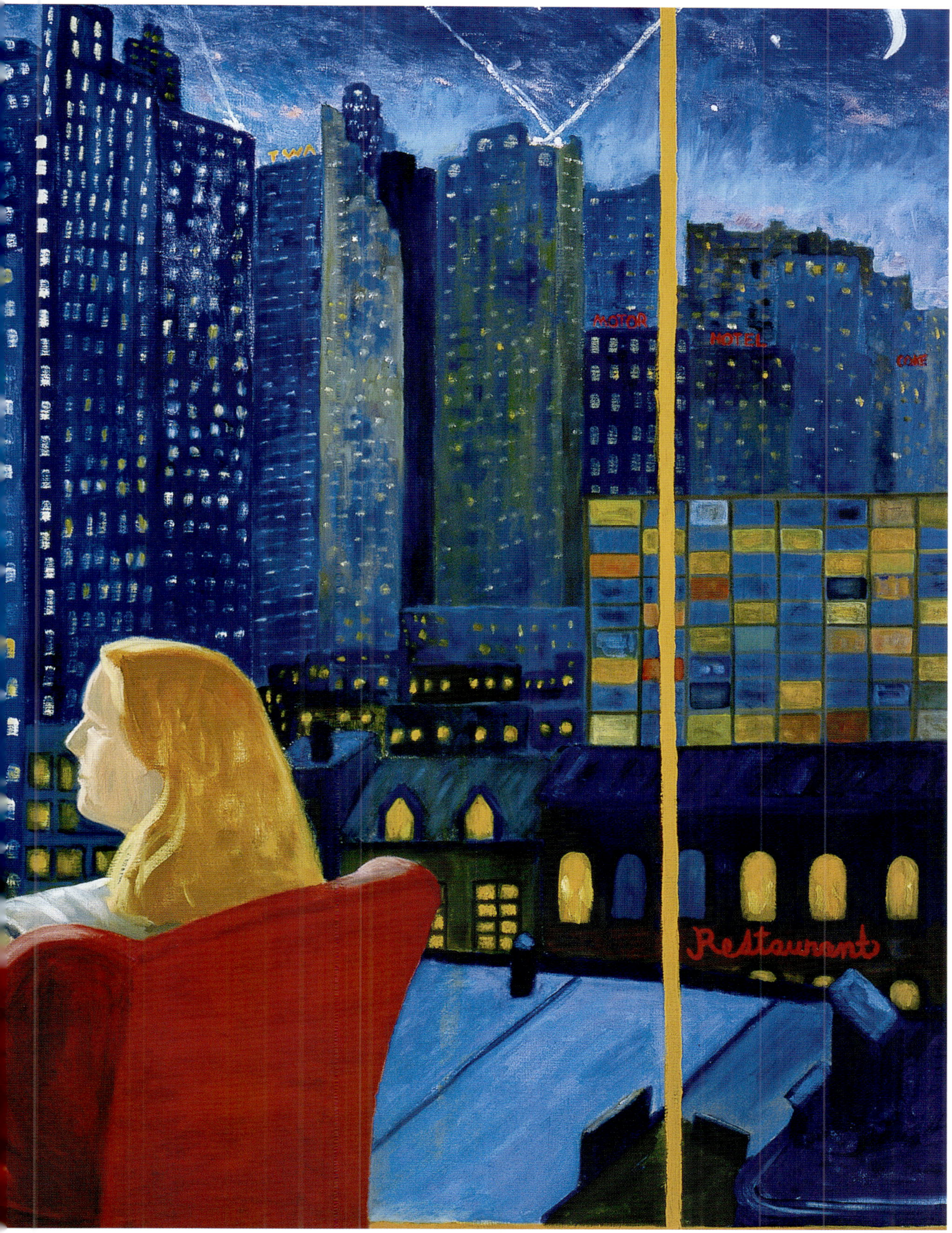
TWA
MOTOR
HOTEL
Restaurant

Kroch's & Brentano's

CHICAGO, ILLINOIS

In Chicago, one of the venerable bookselling institutions for years was Kroch's & Brentano's. Kroch's was opened in the early part of the twentieth century by Adolph Kroch and was later managed by his son Carl Kroch. In the early 1930s, Kroch's bought Brentano's and made the Kroch's Chicago-area stores into one of the nation's most vital retail bookselling institutions by the early 1960s. The store on Wabash, under the "El" train, was Kroch's flagship location and one of America's foremost bookselling centers for well over fifty years. Several very notable booksellers were associated with this store, including Wendell Goodpasture, Bill McCarthy, Doris Laufer, and Bill Rickman.

I first visited the Kroch's & Brentano's store on a hot summer night in 1960. I recall the heat and humidity, the traffic, the elevated train roaring overhead. I ducked into the bookstore for a respite of cool air and quiet, and I have always remembered the civility of the place. On other visits to Chicago over the years, I always went into the store and was reminded of my first visit. My last visit was shortly before the store closed in 1995, marking a definite conclusion to a magnificent period of Chicago bookselling.

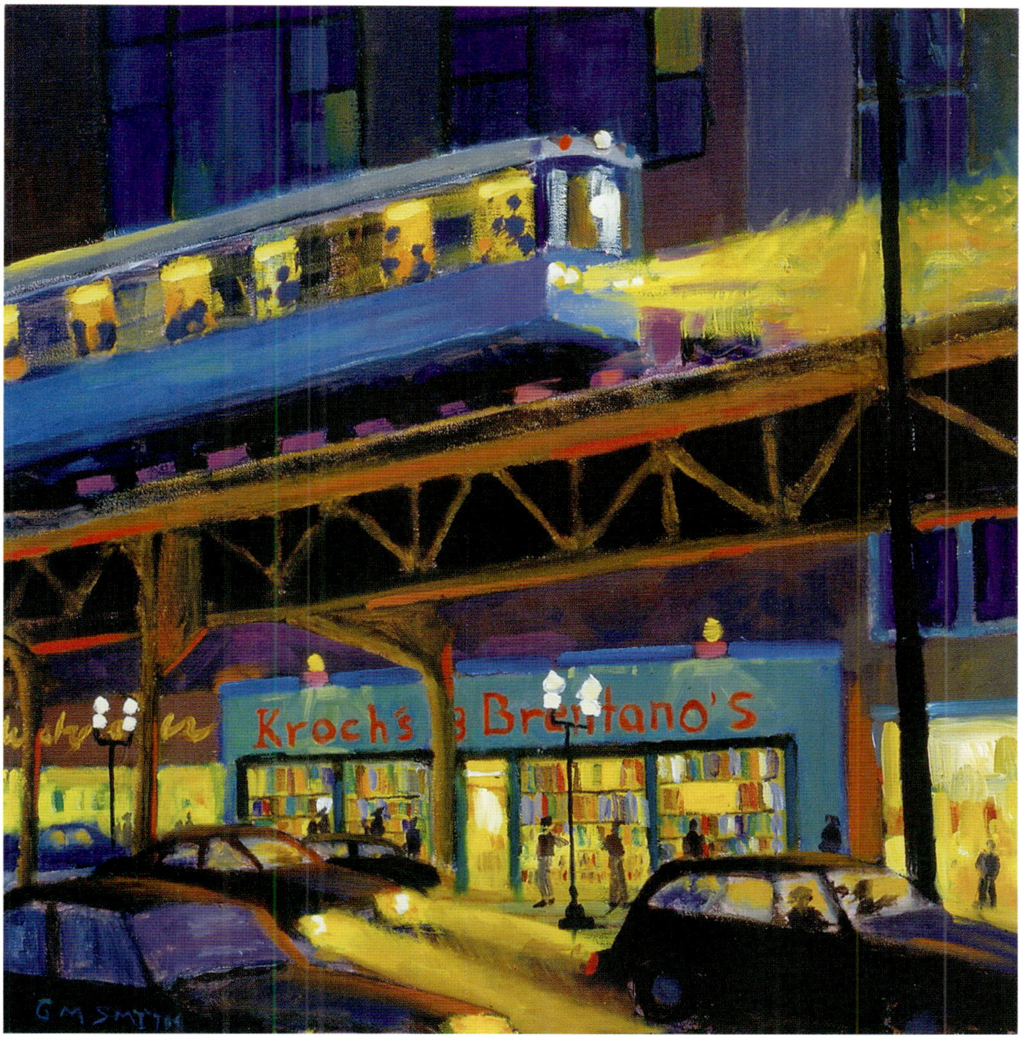

Gibbs M. Smith, Kroch's & Brentano's Bookstore, December Rush Hour on Wabash Avenue, Chicago, *1996. Oil on linen, 16" × 20".*

Bank Street Bookstore

NEW YORK CITY

Bank Street Bookstore opened in 1970 in a small space in the lobby of the Bank Street College. Originally intended to serve the needs of the college community, the bookstore's success soon necessitated a move to a larger location near Columbia University, on the corner of Broadway and West 112th Street, to accommodate the steady stream of customers composed of students, parents, and educators alike.

Over the course of several years, the bookstore has expanded to create more space to house an extensive list of both fiction and nonfiction titles along with a marvelous selection of children's books, learning games, toys, classroom supplies, and audio and video materials. The staff are constantly expanding their own reading lists so they can help each customer find just the right book.

One of my favorite things to do in Manhattan is to visit Columbia University and then walk down to Bank Street Bookstore. As we have developed our children's book line at Gibbs Smith, Publisher, I have always found inspiration and stimulating ideas there.

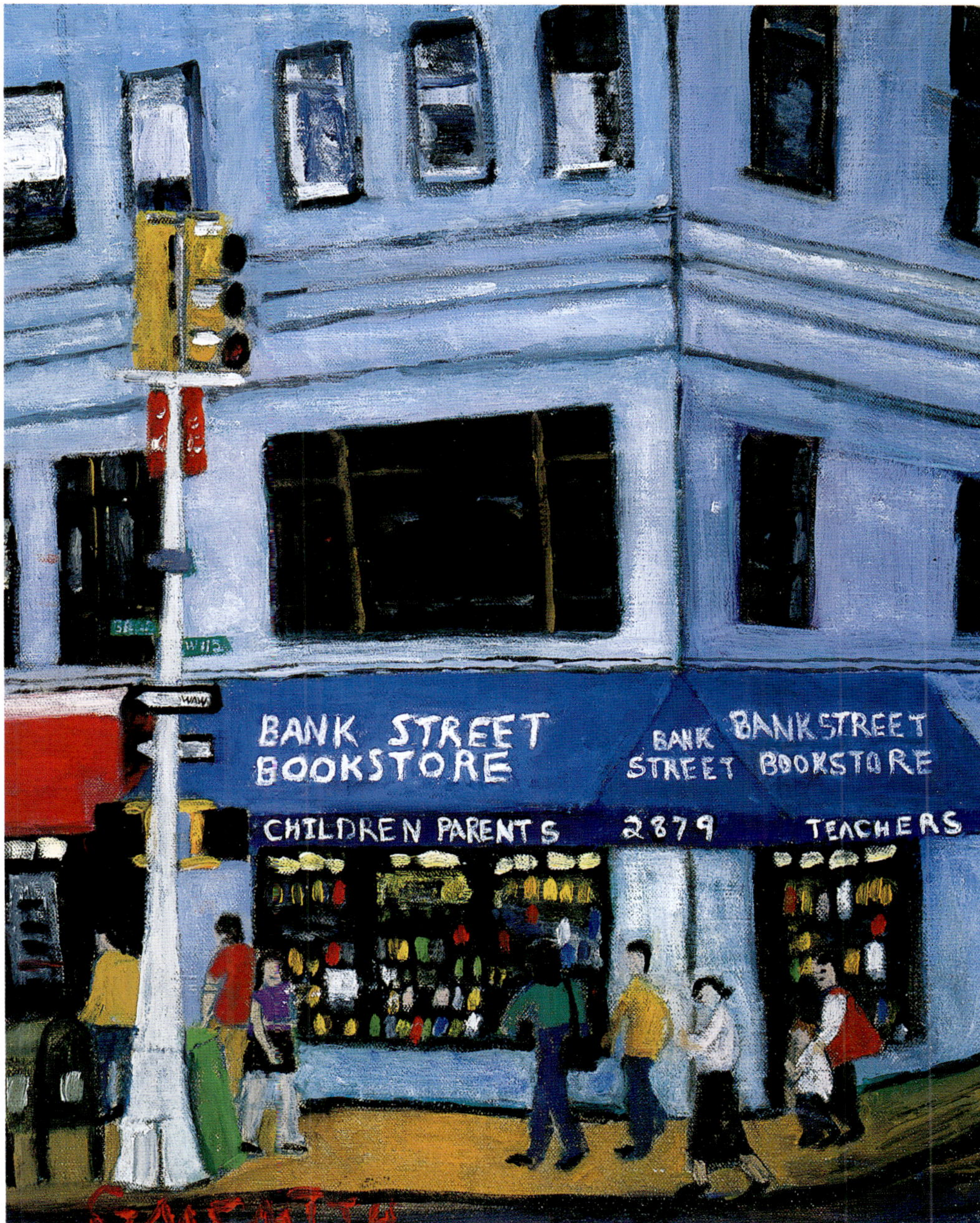

Gibbs M. Smith, Bank Street Bookstore, New York, *2005. Oil on canvas, 18" × 24".*

Barnes & Noble at Union Square

NEW YORK CITY

by Steve Riggio, CEO of Barnes & Noble, Inc.

Bookselling is, of course, a vocation, but it is also an avocation, an art, and a passion. Like our publishing partners at Gibbs Smith, we at Barnes & Noble view ourselves as creative participants in a community that links authors and readers.

We were deeply pleased when artist/publisher Gibbs Smith chose to honor us by painting a Barnes & Noble store. We were doubly gratified when we learned that the subject was our Union Square bookstore. This towering Beaux Arts structure is not only our flagship store; in many ways, it exemplifies the continuity and traditions of our shared mission; in the words of Gibbs Smith, Publisher, "to enrich and inspire humankind."

The magnificent Queen Anne style building that our bookstore occupies is the Century Building, formerly the home of *Century Magazine*, *Century Publishing Company*, and *Saint Nicholas*' children's magazine. For several decades, many of the finest authors and artists in America roamed its high-ceilinged rooms, mingling with their editors. Walt Whitman, Stephen Crane, Edith Wharton, Frederic Remington, and N. C. Wyeth were just a few of the prominent contributors to the publications. Even Ulysses S. Grant and Theodore Roosevelt were Century authors.

If you walk through our Union Square store these days, you might spot a young poet heading towards the registers with a copy of *Leaves of Grass* or a new bestseller. Head upstairs and you might be treated to a live event featuring Nick Hornby or John Grisham; Toni Morrison or Don DeLillo; a poet laureate or a rock star; a White House occupant, past or future. One night, we even hosted an upstart author named Barack Obama.

Like Gibbs Smith, we at Barnes & Noble find that what continues and what sustains us is our commitment to connecting writers and artists to readers.

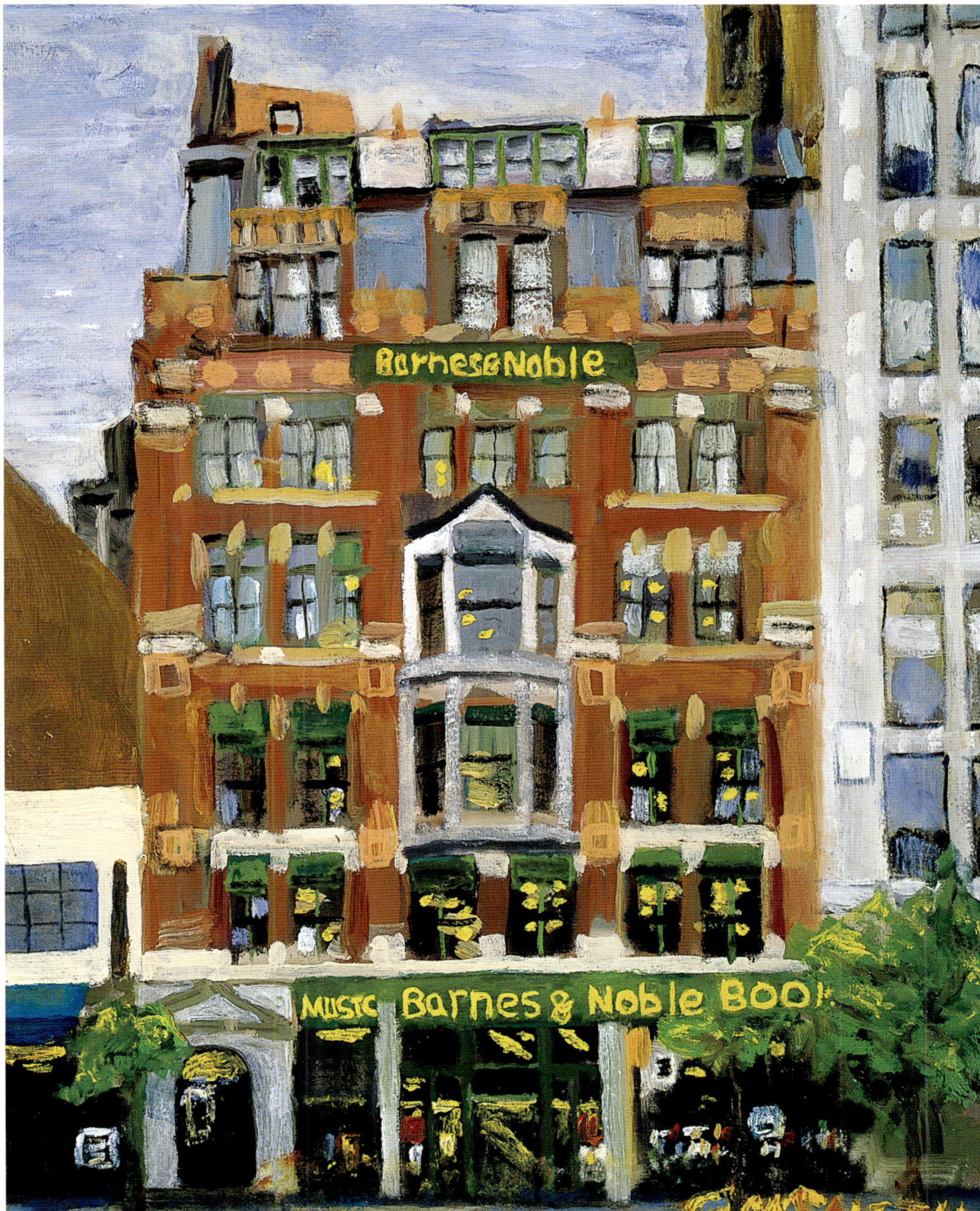

Gibbs M. Smith, Bookstore, Union Square, New York, *1997. Oil on linen, 16" × 20".*

Strand Book Store

NEW YORK CITY

A visit to Strand is one of the greatest bookstore experiences our nation affords. I always love the feeling of anticipation and excitement as I walk through its doors. Strand was founded by Benjamin Bass in 1927 and is now operated by his son Fred and Fred's daughter, Nancy. Fred began working in the store at the age of thirteen and took over as manager in 1956. A few years later, he moved the store from its original location on New York's "Book Row"—located on Fourth Street and once home to forty-eight bookstores—to its current location on Broadway and 12th Street.

Today Strand is the only survivor of Book Row, and the store continues to thrive in spite of the plight of independent bookstores, thanks in big part to its huge inventory. Strand is home to literally millions of books. It offers thousands of new titles at a discount and has an impressive collection of used books, including the largest collection of rare books in New York. One could spend days there, searching for that great find or stumbling upon it while merely browsing. You never know what a visit to Strand will turn up.

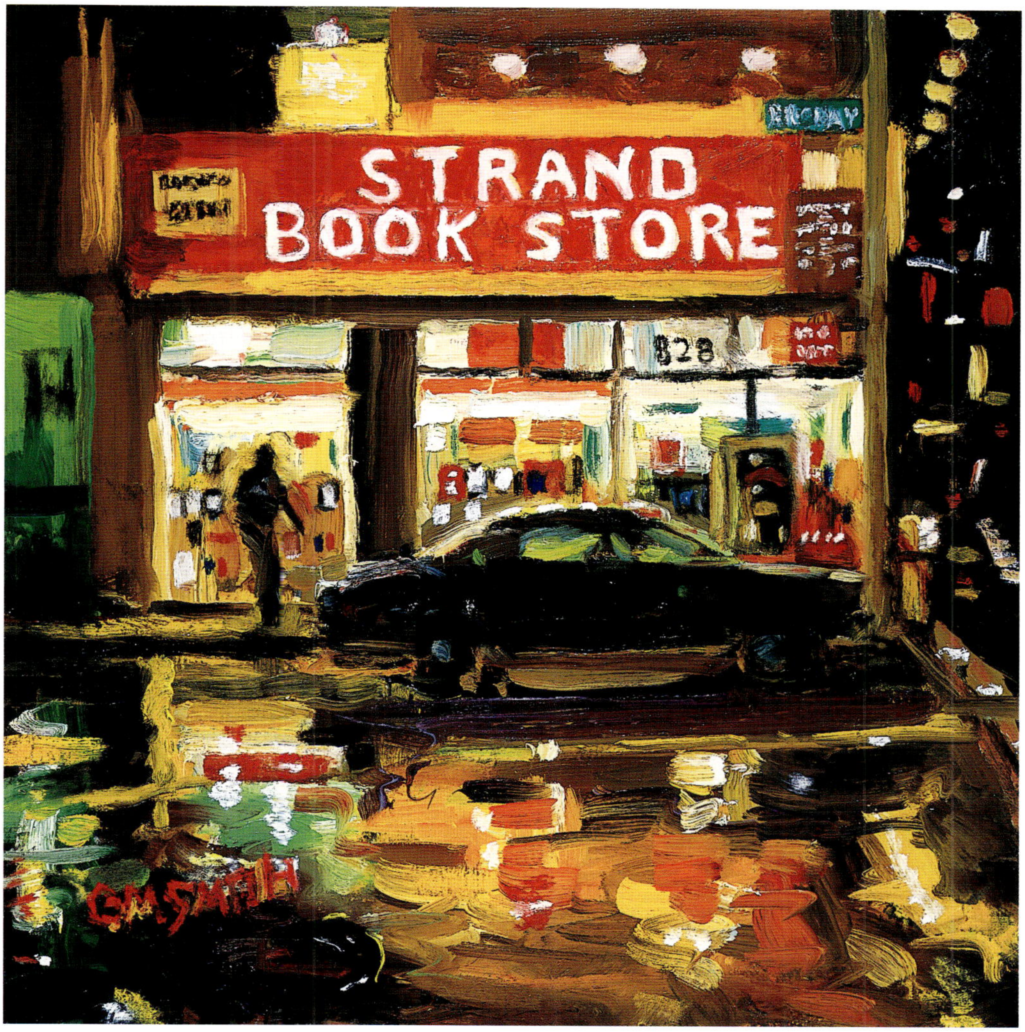

Gibbs M. Smith, Strand Book Store in the Rain, *2003. Oil on linen, 16" × 16".*

Book Soup

LOS ANGELES, CALIFORNIA

Book Soup Bookstore, located on the Sunset Strip in West Hollywood, California, has been serving the Los Angeles book community since it first opened in 1975. I visit there regularly when I travel to the Los Angeles area and am always rewarded by its stimulating spirit and exciting collection of books.

As one of the last large independent bookstores, with over sixty thousand titles in stock, Book Soup caters to the specialized interests of their clientele with a diverse inventory of literary fiction, nonfiction, film, art, music, photography, and more. The store is as famous for its high profile signing events—which have featured authors and celebrities including Gore Vidal, Edward Albee, and Robert Wagner—as it is for its walls of bookshelves piled from floor to ceiling. There is virtually something for everyone to be found in this wonderful store.

Glenn Goldman, who founded Book Soup in 1975, passed away in January 2009. After his passing, there was an outpouring of affection by customers, staff, authors, colleagues, and the community, who remembered a kind, smart, generous, wryly humorous man whose dedication to contributing books and culture to his community was appreciated and treasured.

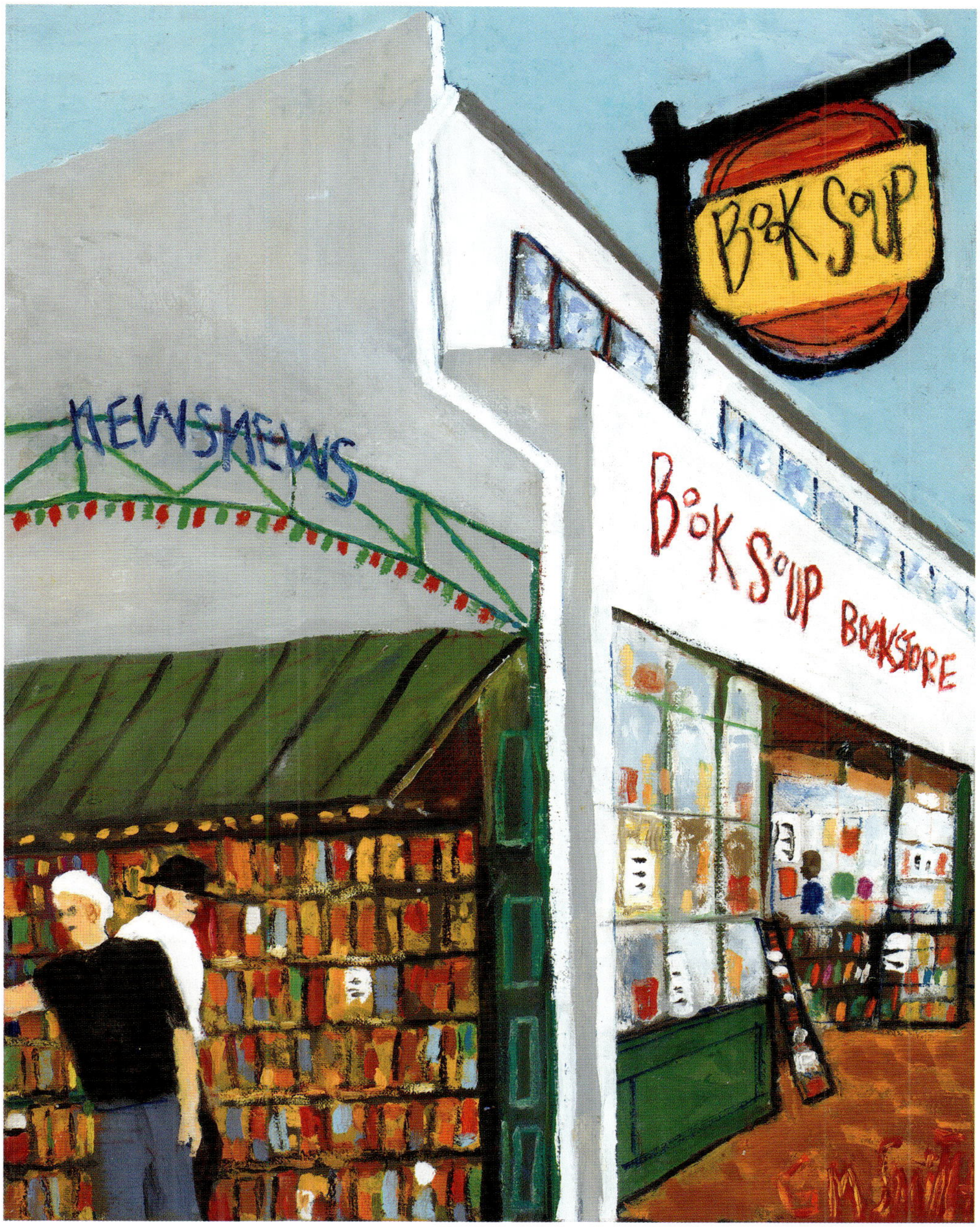

Gibbs M. Smith, Bookstore, Hollywood, *2008. Oil on linen, 16" × 20".*

Books & Co.

NEW YORK CITY

Founded in 1978 by Jeanette Watson, this two-level, brick-walled, wood-shelved store was best known for fostering great writers and for its intelligent, diverse collection of hard-to-find books on philosophy, poetry, classic literature, and art, as well as popular bestsellers. Locals and celebrities alike treasured it for its atmosphere of sophistication and literary cachet. Eminent writers and playwrights (Jacques Derrida, Susan Sontag, Kurt Vonnegut, Truman Capote, Neil Simon, and Sam Shepard, to name a few) gave readings there or shopped there or both, and famous actors and musicians also browsed the shelves. The "Wall," covered in thoughtfully selected works, was a veritable Who's Who of literature.

Books & Co. closed in 1997 amid great protests from writers and loyal customers.

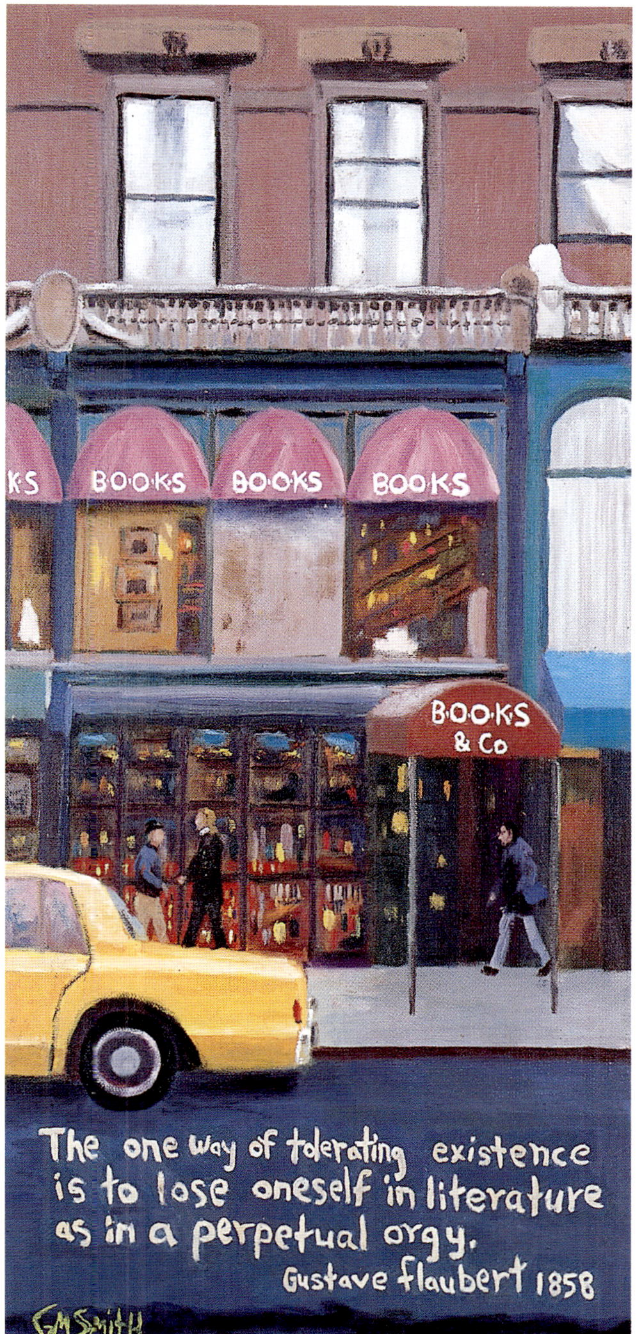

Gibbs M. Smith, Jeanette's Bookstore, New York, *1994. Oil on linen, 16" × 20".*

Borders

ANN ARBOR, MICHIGAN

Borders began in Ann Arbor in the early 1970s. Those familiar with the company at its beginnings say that Tom Borders was teaching at the University of Michigan and Louis Borders was a computer specialist/grad student at MIT. Louis moved to Ann Arbor where his brother Tom was living. The apartment he rented was filled with used books that had been abandoned by the previous resident. Tom and Louis started selling the books and enjoyed it. They evolved it into a business. Used books ultimately gave way to new books, which gave the Borders brothers more control to ensure availability of any specific title sought by customers. Being a computer specialist, Louis then devised one of the first computerized inventory control systems for any retailer anywhere in the country. It permitted the Borders brothers to leverage the inventory investment of their small bookstore into an extensive title base at relatively small cost. They were able to differentiate their store from the many local bookstores throughout Ann Arbor by delivering a huge title selection to the information-hungry faculty, administration, and students at the University of Michigan, as well as to native Ann Arborites. Why Ann Arbor? That's where Tom and Louis lived, and books were what the community loved.

Early on, the store was located at 303 S. State Street, where it resided for about twenty years. In the early 1990s, Borders arranged to relocate into a space that had been occupied by Jacobson's department store because of its larger quarters. The brick exterior of the current location was initially built to house Jacobson's. Borders opened up the exterior by adding windows and awnings, while reconfiguring the interior to its own needs.

Since that first Borders store opened, the company has grown to more than 1,000 Borders and Waldenbooks stores. Borders has embraced the technology age, opening "concept stores," which offer downloading of music, audio books, and other digital media; personal publishing, such as photo books; and interactive kiosks for exploring travel, cooking, and wellness media.

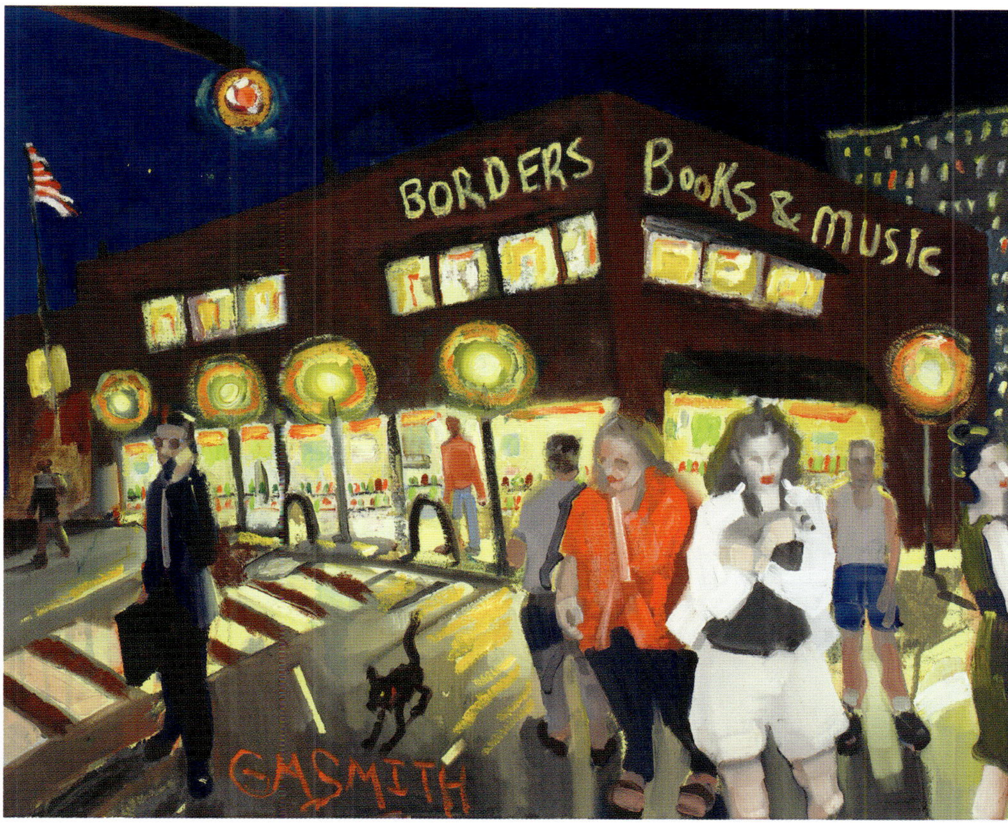

Gibbs M. Smith, Store #1 at Night, *2008. Oil on linen, 16" × 20".*

Broadway Books

PORTLAND, OREGON

Founded in 1992 by Gloria Borg Olds and Roberta Dyer, Broadway Books is a great neighborhood bookstore located in northeast Portland. Strong selections of contemporary literary fiction, biography, and Judaica line the shelves, along with a good selection of regular bestselling titles.

Broadway Books is proud of its continued connection to the community it serves. The store hosts readings by both local and national touring authors and is involved in fund-raising activities and literacy programs, supporting local writers and students.

I would be the most content if my children grew up to be the kind of people who think decorating consists mostly of building enough bookshelves.

—Anna Quindlen

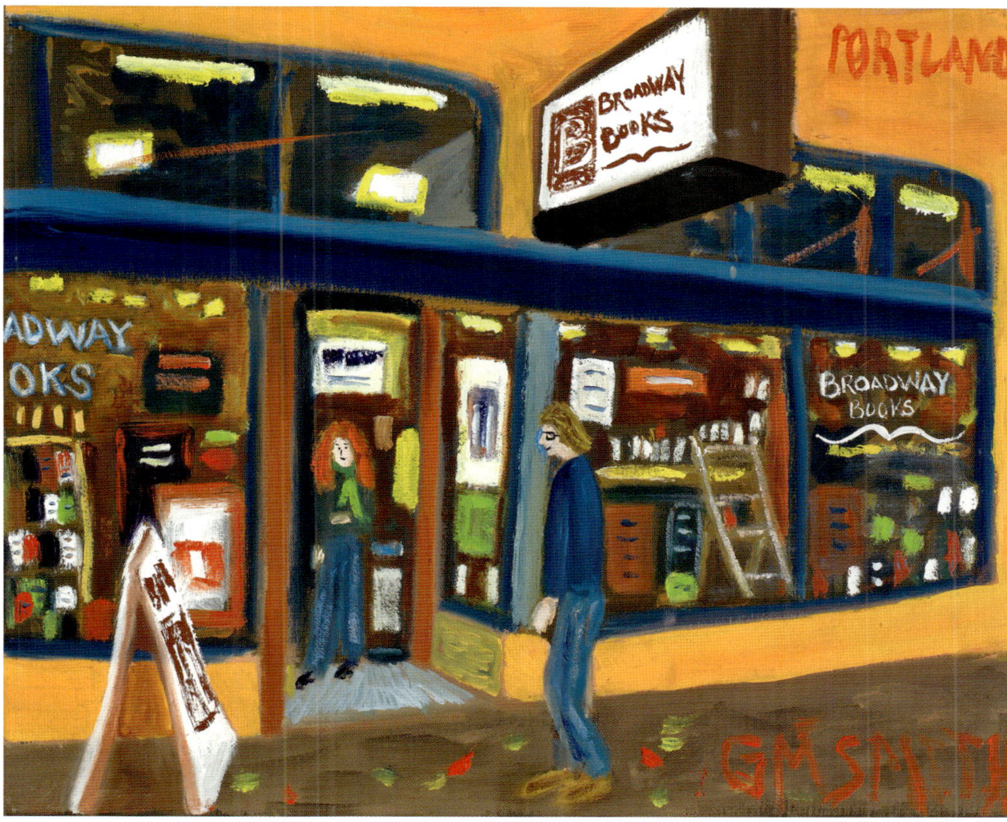

Gibbs M. Smith, Autumn Afternoon in Portland, *2009. Oil on linen, 16" × 20".*

Chapters: A Literary Bookstore

WASHINGTON, D.C.

Chapters, founded in 1985 and owned by Terri Merz and Robin Diener, is an elegant and personal store, an oasis of civility. Its program of readings by internationally respected authors gives the store the aura of a literary salon. The passions, tastes, and enthusiasms of the owners are reflected in their wide range and selection of books that begins with an immense poetry section, literary fiction old and new, literature in foreign languages, the culinary arts, children's literature, natural history, and more, catering to serious readers and browsers alike. They also host many other activities, such as the annual Marcel Proust birthday celebration, the annual George Eliot memorial lecture, and a celebration of Anthony Powell's *Dance to the Music of Time,* in which I have been privileged to participate. The store's slogan, from Horace, is "Littera Scripta Manet" (the written letter remains).

In 2007, Chapters started the nonprofit Chapters Literary Arts Center as an addition to the bookstore. The center is dedicated to preserving literary culture and reducing illiteracy in the community through programs at the store as well as off-site locations.

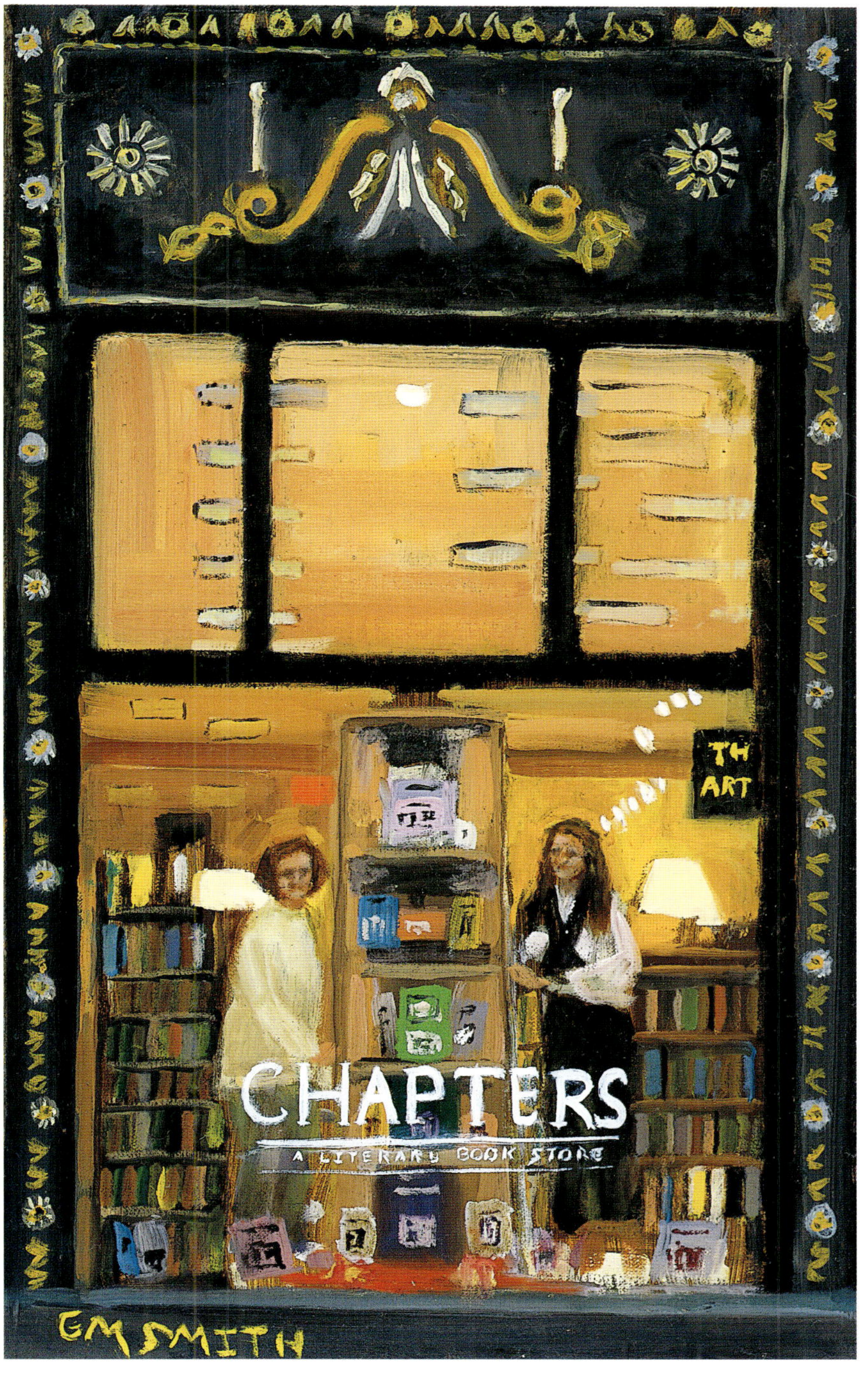

Gibbs M. Smith, Chapters, *1996. Oil on linen, 16" × 20".*

Chaucer's Books

SANTA BARBARA, CALIFORNIA

Chaucer's Books opened in 1974 and I've been visiting the store ever since, whenever I am in the area. It was founded by Mahri Kerley, who is regularly recognized as one of California's legendary book people. This is one of the most successful independent bookstores in California and has a very loyal clientele.

Chaucer's has a strong literary offering including many British and Canadian imports and academic titles not usually found in bookstores off university campuses. Chaucer's also serves as a source for local interest such as history and nature.

I cannot live without books.

—Thomas Jefferson

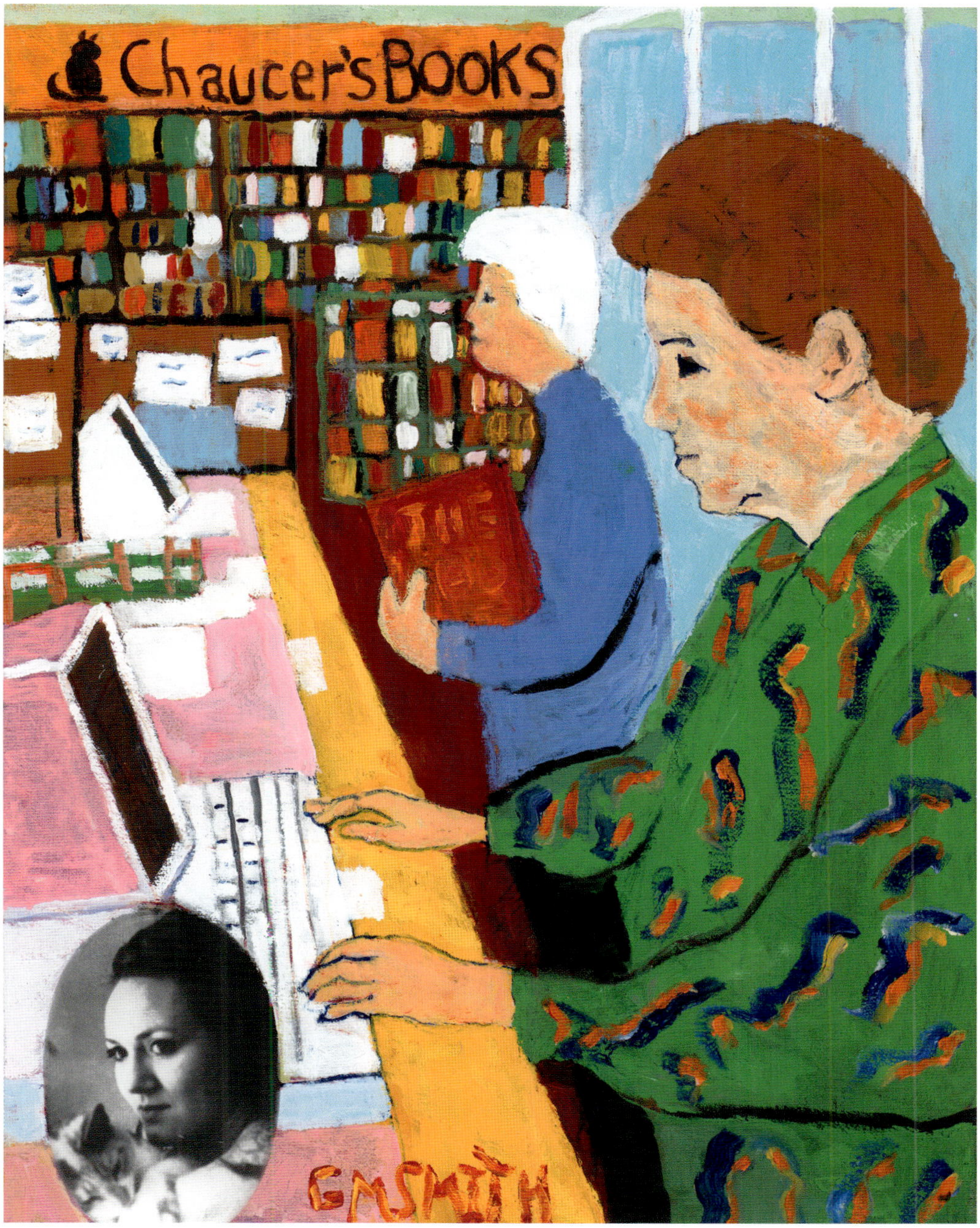

Gibbs M. Smith, Santa Barbara Bookstore, *2006. Oil on linen, 16" × 20".*

Christopher's Books

SAN FRANCISCO, CALIFORNIA

Christopher's Books was founded in 1991 by Christopher Ellison, a wonderful man from New Zealand. Located on Potrero Hill in San Francisco, the space occupied by the bookstore originally housed an old-fashioned pharmacy. The shop is only 650 square feet, and many of the original pharmacy fixtures are still intact and used as book displays. The entrance is on a street corner where French doors invite the public to come in and browse. Mr. Ellison returned to New Zealand in 1994 to operate a small dairy farm. The bookstore is now owned and operated by Tee Minot, who has managed the store since 1994.

The Potrero Hill community is passionate about books and has been very supportive of this well-stocked, well-staffed, corner bookshop. Christopher's has become a fixture in the community and is one of my favorite bookstores in San Francisco.

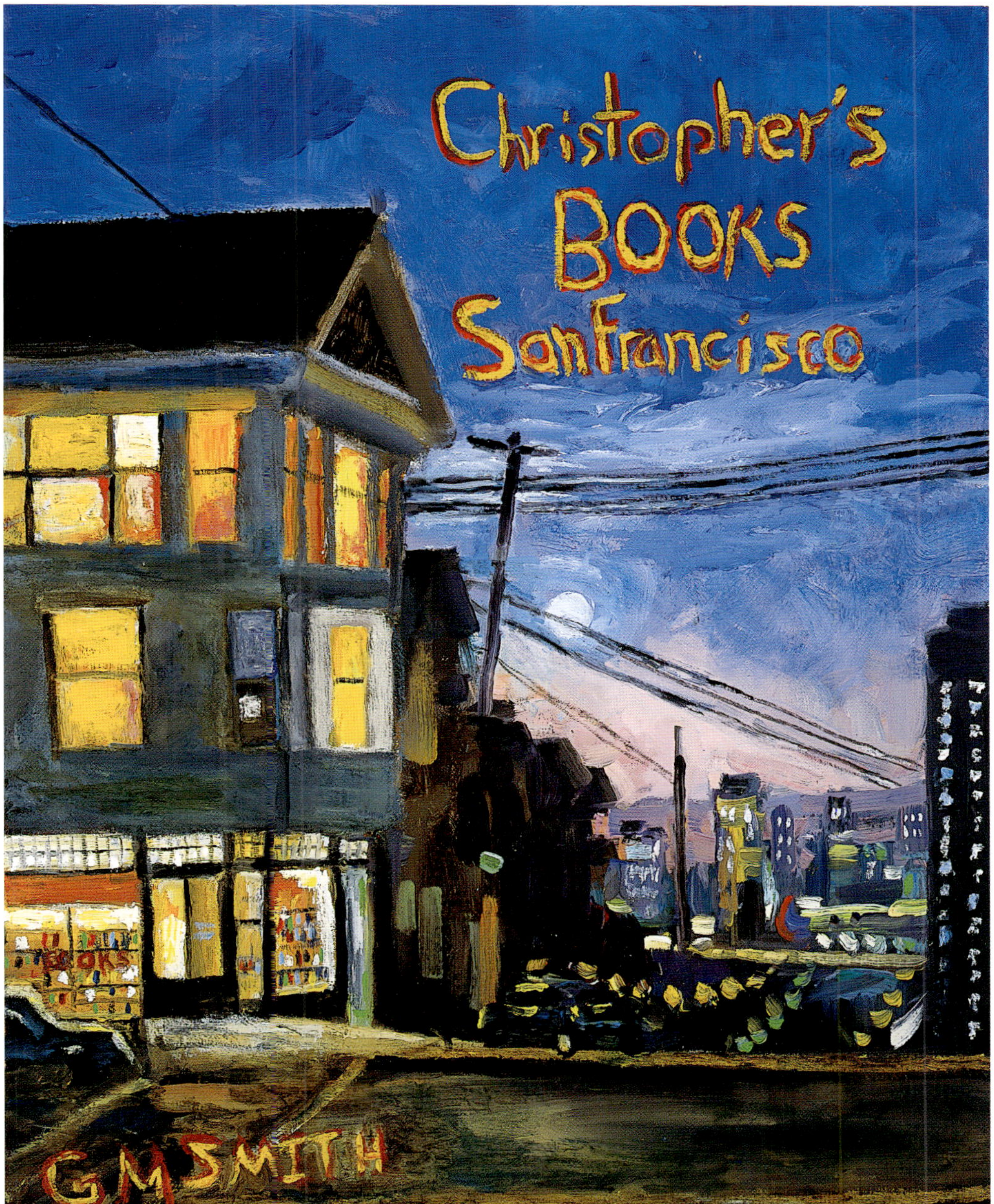

Gibbs M. Smith, Autumn Evening on Potrero Hill, *2004. Oil on linen, 16" × 20".*

City Lights Books

SAN FRANCISCO, CALIFORNIA

Founded in 1953 by Lawrence Ferlinghetti and Peter D. Martin, City Lights is a historic literary hangout that has attracted dynamic individuals and promoted freedom of thoughts and ideas ever since it opened.

City Lights' regulars over the years have included Jack Kerouac and poet Allen Ginsberg, and the store helped to establish new guidelines regarding freedom of speech after publishing Ginsberg's poem "Howl" and successfully defending the work in court.

City Lights' large inventory of books reflects its support of progressive ideas and artistic freedom. The staff makes an effort to promote non-mainstream, thought-provoking titles, from gender studies to world literature to theological debate and much more. The store's selection of poetry and small press books is particularly impressive.

City Lights has been part of my life since the 1960s when I first visited as a college student to discover the beat poets in North Beach. One of my fondest memories of City Lights is walking upstairs to meet with Lawrence in his office, which is situated above the bookstore, passing numerous emblems of Charlie Chaplin along the way. From there we would sometimes walk up Columbus Avenue to the old USA Café and have lunch. We would also discuss the history of the building that City Lights occupies and our shared interest in the art world. Years later, Lawrence gave me my first show as a painter, exhibiting my work on the walls of the bookstore.

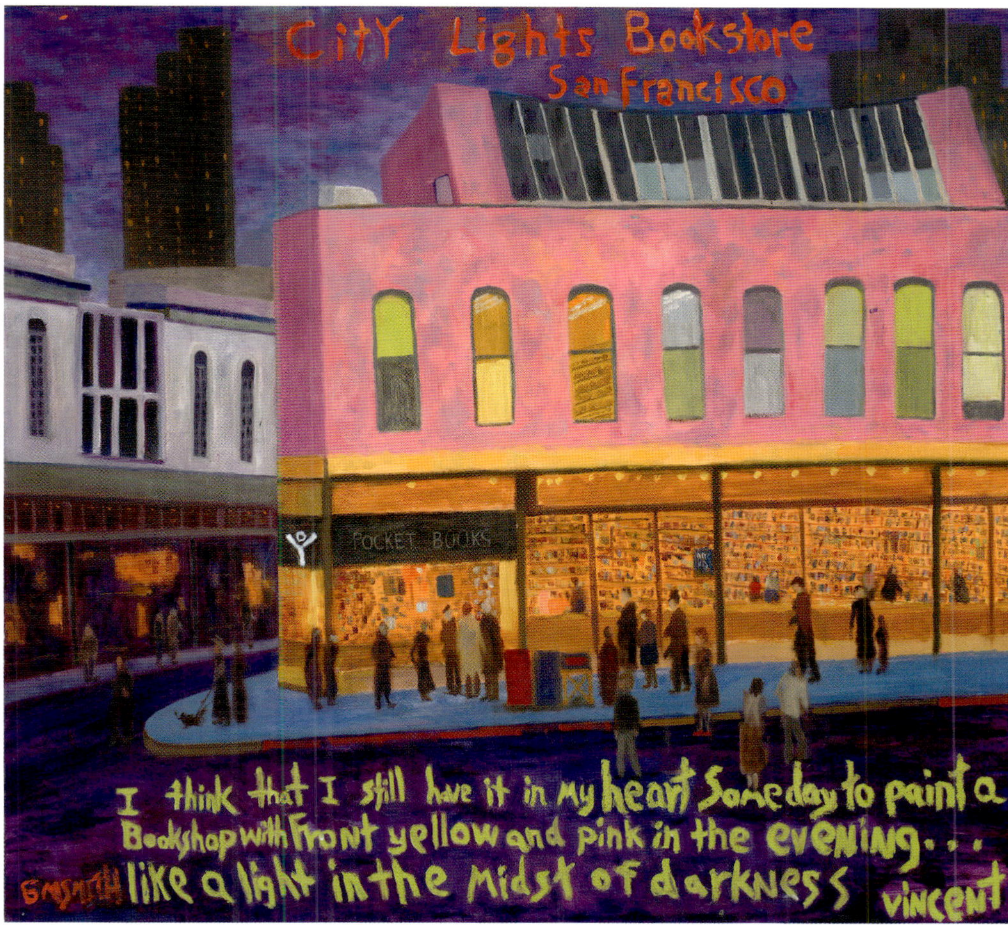

Gibbs M. Smith, City Lights Bookstore, *1988. Oil on canvas, 36" × 40".*

Cody's Books

BERKELEY, CALIFORNIA

by Roger Moss, publishers' representative

In the summer of 1958, when I moved to Berkeley to go to college, Fred Cody was already well ensconced in his tiny paperback bookshop on Euclid Avenue, half a block north of the University of California campus. The store was much too small for all the books Fred had in it, so he had stacks of overstock tucked away high up toward the ceiling above the store's bookshelves. Fred, always energetic, was constantly up and down his ladder getting inaccessible books down so they could be seen. The first book I bought in Berkeley was in his shop. It was *Magic, Science & Religion* by Bronislaw Malikowski in the old Anchor edition.

Fred and Pat, his wife and partner in business and life, were pioneers in the field of selling serious paperback books to serious readers. The post–World War II G.I. Bill had educated millions of vets from working middle-class backgrounds like Fred and brought them into the middle class. They were independent readers. They avoided the stuffy old 'carriage trade' bookstores that disdained the new paperbacks. These were the ideal customers for Fred and Pat, and—fortunately—publishers were turning out plenty of books for this burgeoning market.

Fred and Pat in Berkeley, Roy Kepler in Menlo Park, Lawrence Ferlinghetti in San Francisco, and Herb Beckman in Sausalito created vital and exciting institutions for the dissemination of the ideas their books held, paperback bookstores that were to be models for similar stores that soon spread across the country.

Cody's Books eventually moved into bigger quarters on Telegraph Avenue, a much livelier neighborhood south of the campus, first into an old building with well-worn pine floors at 2476 Telegraph Avenue and later into a new building at the corner of Telegraph and Haste. (This is the store in Gibbs Smith's painting.) However, it was not the location of the store that was important, but the vitality and excitement that Fred

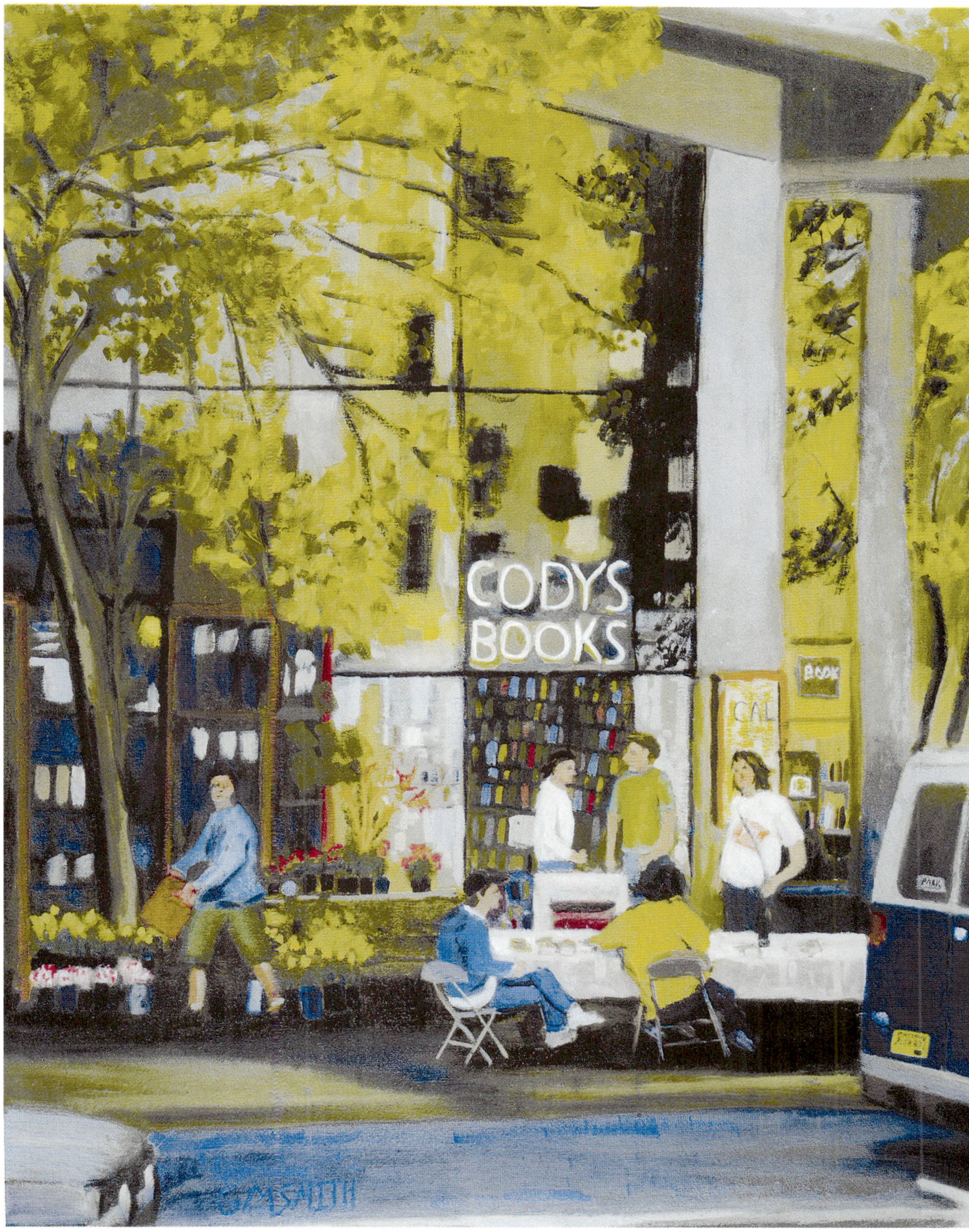

Gibbs M. Smith, Bookstore on Telegraph Avenue, Berkeley, *1989. Oil on linen, 16" × 20".*

and Pat brought to selling books. Fred's favorite job in the store was tearing open the boxes of new titles sent by the publishers. He needed to have the new books and the intellectual excitement they represented front and center in the store. Pat was an ideal partner. Well centered with an understanding of economics and finance, she managed the unglamorous business side of the business, a side so often neglected by idealistic booksellers.

Cody's became a community center as well as a bookstore, and when the troubles came to Berkeley in the 1960s with the police and National Guard clubbing and teargassing antiwar protesters right outside the front door of the shop, it was only natural that Fred not only provided sanctuary to the protesters but also made connections with others in the city and at the university to address the underlying causes of the discord.

Fred was not the only community activist in the family. Pat has had a long and distinguished second career (when not minding the books at Cody's) in speaking out in defense of women's rights and especially on women's health issues and the abuses of the drug companies.

Fred and Pat sold their store in 1977, but the story of Cody's Books was not over. Andy Ross, the new owner, managed the store capably for another thirty years. He expanded the size of the store and its inventory. He introduced computerized inventory control and accounting practices to the store. He opened two satellite stores, one in Berkeley and one in San Francisco. It was under Andy's stewardship in 1989 that the store suffered a firebomb, retaliation for the prominent display that Andy had given to Salman Rushdie's *The Satanic Verses*, a novel under fatwa from Iranian clerics. The day after the bomb exploded—concerned for the safety of his staff—Andy held a meeting of his employees to get their advice about the future. They voted unanimously to continue to stock and display the controversial book, an act in protection of the First Amendment and of the public's unfettered right to read.

With this rich history of social activism uppermost in my mind it was difficult for me to attend the melancholy get-together in 2006—forty-eight years after I first entered Cody's Books—at the old Telegraph Avenue store when it closed "for good." After so many years of community service, a bookstore like no other, a unique gem, was being lost that day. Within two years the other Cody's locations had closed as well.

There are still people who are so badly adjusted to reality that they insist on either writing books or selling them.

—Fred Cody

Collected Works

SANTA FE, NEW MEXICO

Collected Works is the oldest independently owned bookstore in Santa Fe. Mother-and-daughter team Dorothy Massey and Mary Massey Wolf own the store. The bookshelves, which are under the watchful eyes of "Kitty Carson," their resident feline, store a variety of literature, in particular books related to the history, travel, and architecture of Santa Fe and New Mexico. The store hosts book signings with notable authors, both at the store and during community events.

When I walk into a bookstore, any bookstore, first thing in the morning, I'm flooded with a sense of hushed excitement.

—Lewis Buzbee,
The Yellow-Lighted Bookshop

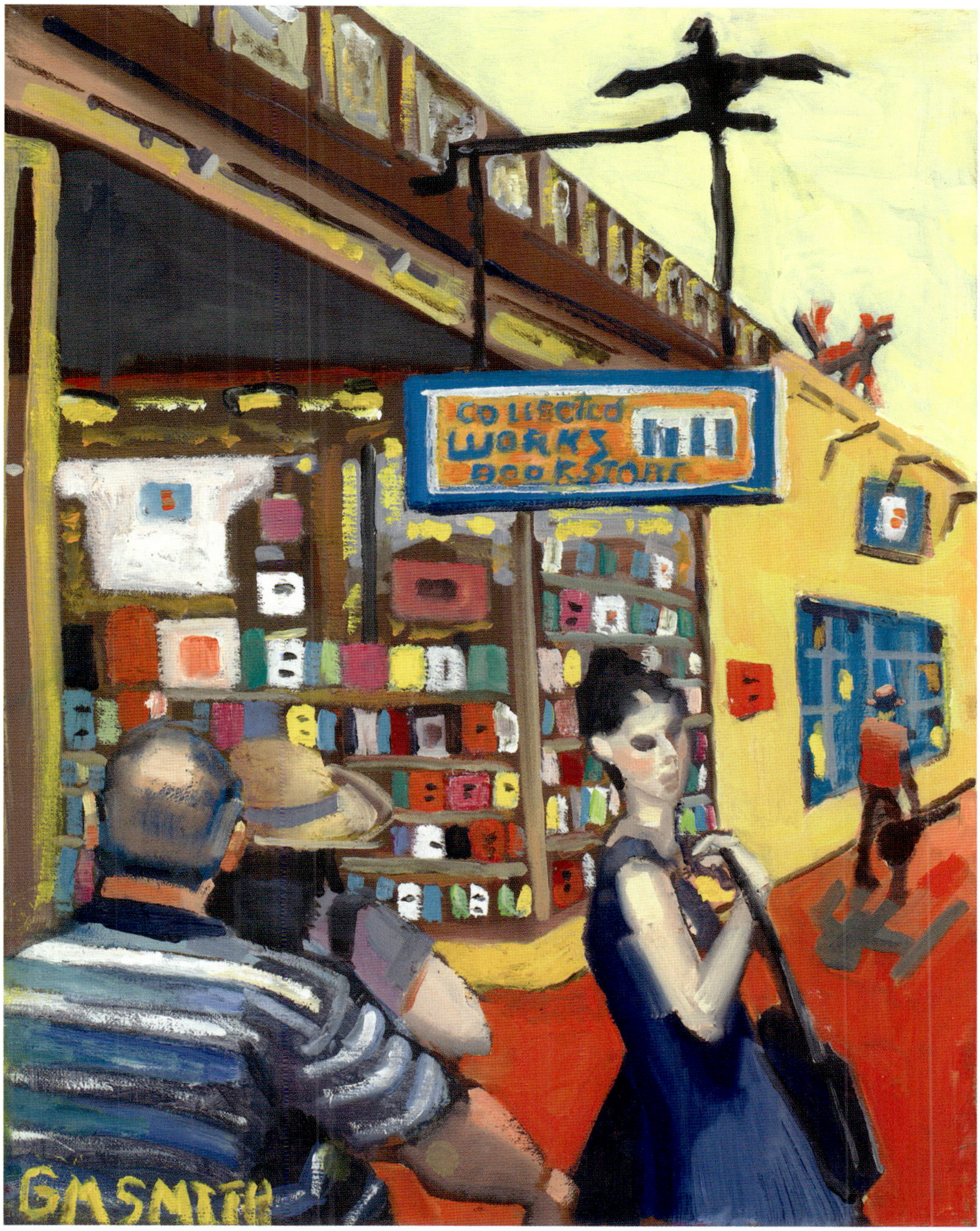

Gibbs M. Smith, Summer Afternoon in Santa Fe, *2009. Oil on linen, 16" × 20".*

The Corner Bookstore

NEW YORK CITY

The Corner Bookstore, owned by Lenny Golay and Ray Sherman, is located on the Upper East Side of Manhattan and offers a friendly staff that is very much involved with its customers. It was also the blueprint for the bookshop featured in the film *You've Got Mail.* This tiny bookstore features an extensive children's collection as well as a wide variety of other titles that includes classics, bestsellers, art, design, architecture, history, poetry, and travel books.

Lord! when you sell a man a book you don't sell just twelve ounces of paper and ink and glue—you sell him a whole new life. Love and friendship and humour and ships at sea by night—there's all heaven and earth in a book, a real book.

—Christopher Morley

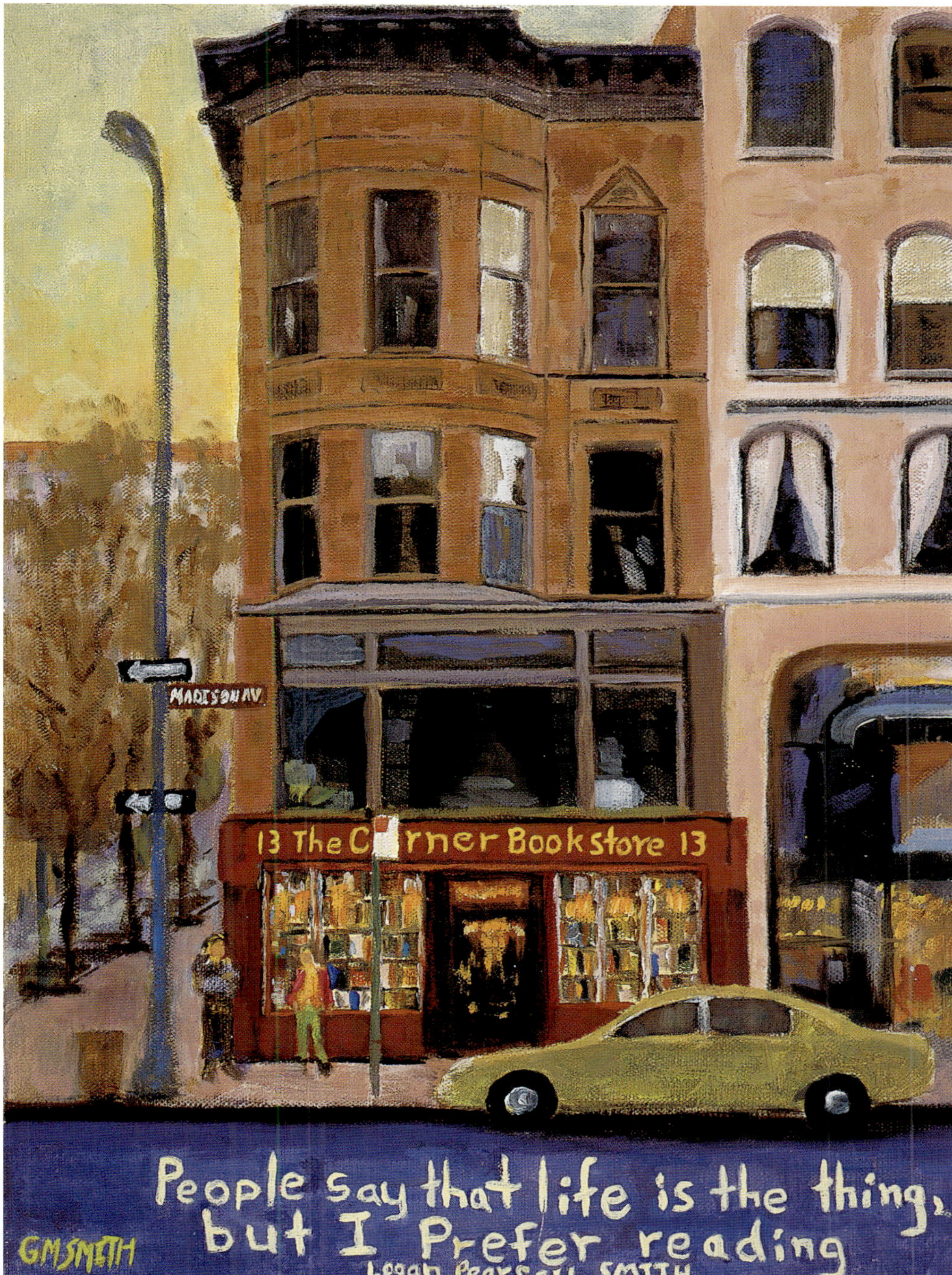

Gibbs M. Smith, Upper East Side, *1996. Oil on linen, 16" × 20".*

The Cottage Book Shop

GLEN ARBOR, MICHIGAN

The Cottage Book Shop resides in a historic cedar log cabin built in the 1920s, located in Glen Arbor, Michigan, on the shores of Lake Michigan and the Sleeping Bear National Lakeshore, which is famous for the world's largest moving sand dune. Owner Barbara Siepker and her staff offer an amazing selection of books and have made their store a vital center of the region.

Barbara Siepker, owner of The Cottage Book Shop:

Being an independent bookstore owner has got to be the world's best job! Where else can you choose books whose stories and ideas you love and wish to personally share with enthusiastic, literate friends—friends we have come to make with authors and customers, who call us their favorite bookstore? In my case, it has also been fun to create a gathering place in a historic log cabin near a scenic national lakeshore that annually hosts a million seasonal visitors. I chose to move this resort log cabin into the center of the village to match the bookstore name, carry local history books displayed in a canoe, and showcase Gibbs Smith design books on rustic cedar shelves to create a special sense of place. What's not to love about bookselling?

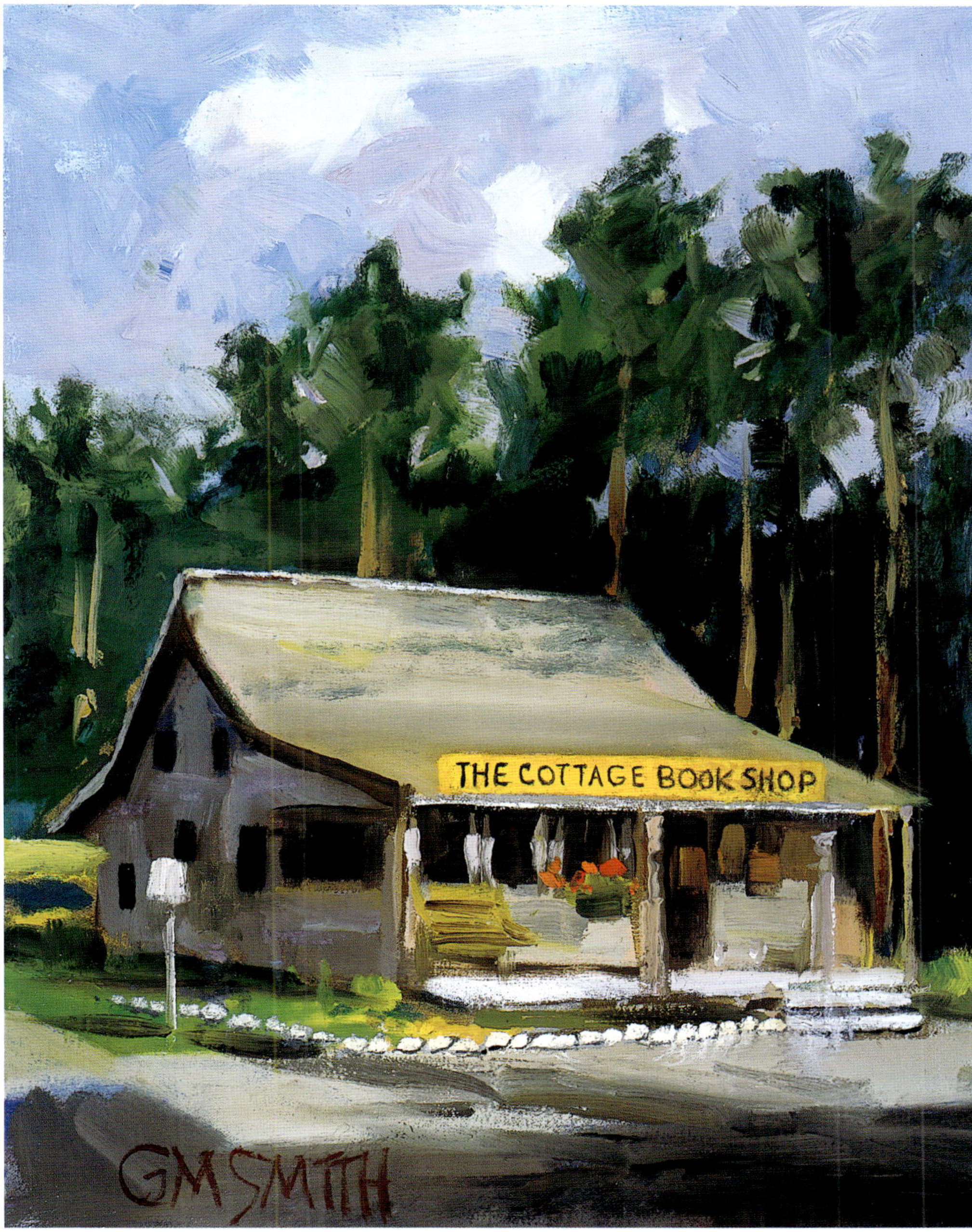

Gibbs M. Smith, On the Shore of Lake Michigan, *2002. Oil on linen, 16" × 20".*

The Depot Bookstore & Café

MILL VALLEY, CALIFORNIA

Family owned and operated, the Depot Bookstore was founded by William and Mary Turnbull in 1987 and is located in a historic railway depot built in 1925 for the Northwest Pacific Railroad. It is a wonderful full-service bookstore that has become a major cultural institution and has enthusiastic community support. The café is a favorite local hangout, where you can sip a latte on the patio while reading the latest bestseller or watching people on the town square. Each month the café features works of a local artist on its walls.

It is a great thing to start life with a small number of really good books which are your very own.

—Sir Arthur Conan Doyle

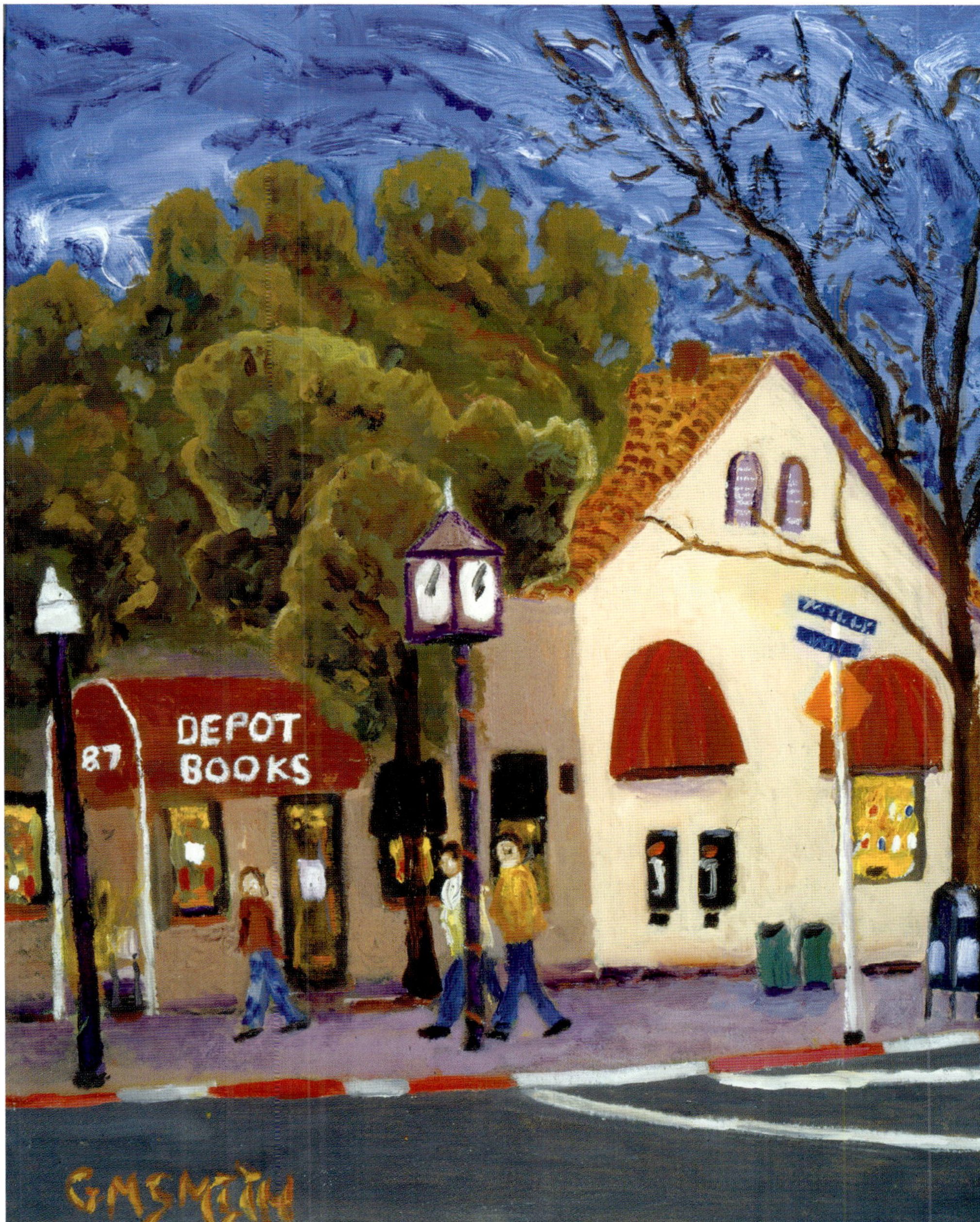

Gibbs M. Smith, Mill Valley Bookstore, *2007. Oil on linen, 16" × 20".*

Shakespeare & Co. Bookstore

NEW YORK CITY

Shakespeare & Co.'s store is located on Broadway in the vibrant neighborhood of NYU. They have more locations in New York, but this is my favorite and I visit it on a regular basis. I was there most recently on a rainy December evening. This painting is my impression of that evening, evoking the warm glow the store gives the neighborhood.

Inside, the lofty shelves are filled with books that represent the interests of this university neighborhood: alternative literature, poetry, theater, film, political science, philosophy, history, women's studies. Shakespeare & Co. has a large selection of play scripts, which actors and theater students in the area greatly appreciate.

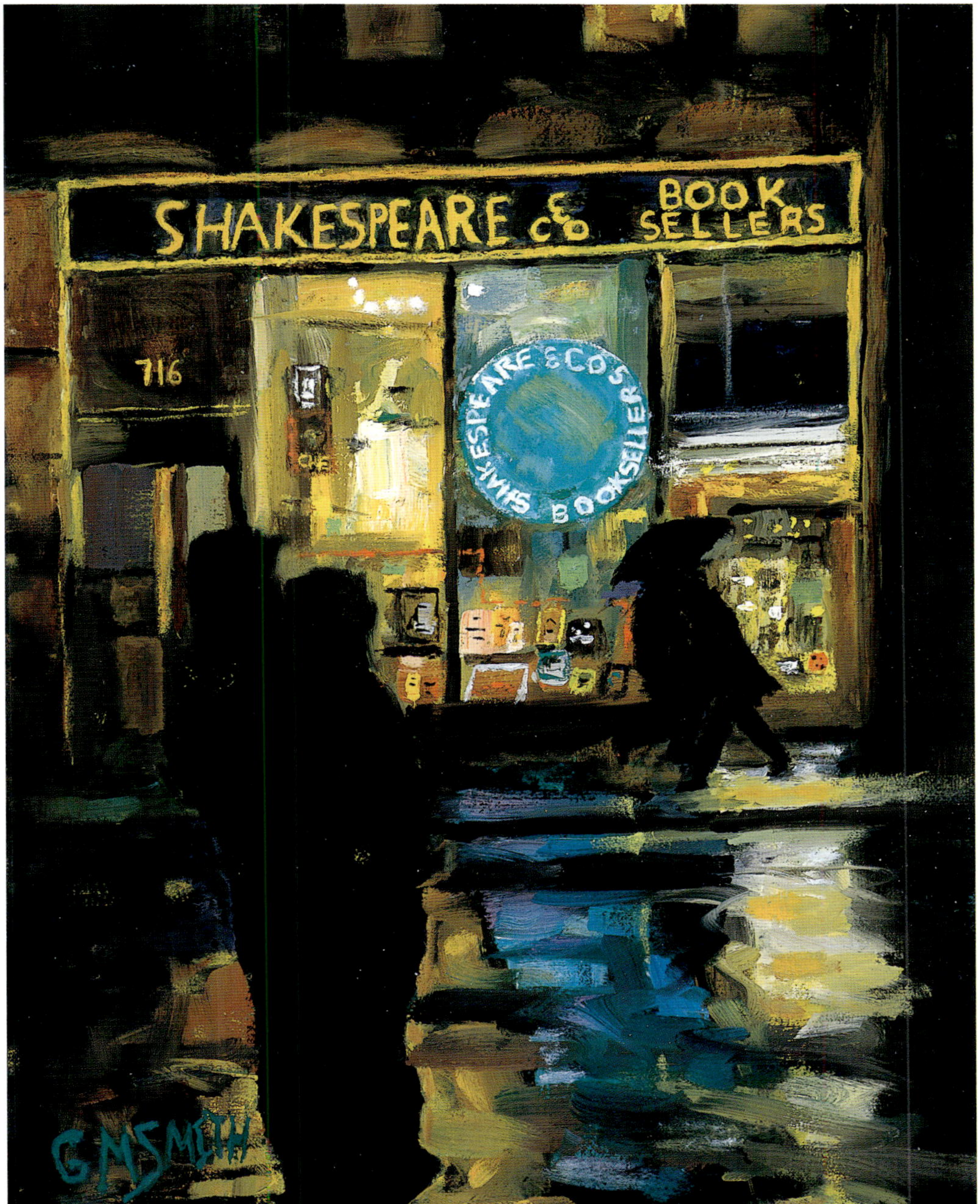

Gibbs M. Smith, Bookstore, Lower Manhattan, *2008. Oil on linen, 16" × 20".*

D.G. Wills Books

LA JOLLA, CALIFORNIA

La Jolla, California, an interesting combination of beachfront town and intellectual center, is home to the Salk Institute and the University of California, San Diego, as well as D.G. Wills. Founded by Dennis Wills in 1979, this fine independent bookstore has a loyal and intellectual clientele. Wills and his carpenter friends have created a marvelous interior—with a redwood beam cathedral ceiling—and exterior that have a distinct personality. Wills hosts hundreds of events each year in the store and has included readings from such writers as Allen Ginsberg, Norman Mailer, and Gore Vidal.

When I was last there, I asked Dennis to characterize the feeling of the store. He described it as a "sort of nineteenth-century cracker barrel hardware store from a John Ford film, with Pabst Blue Ribbon in the refrigerator." The bookstore inventory is jam-packed from floor to ceiling with unique new and old books, with a special emphasis in classical studies, philosophy, and science.

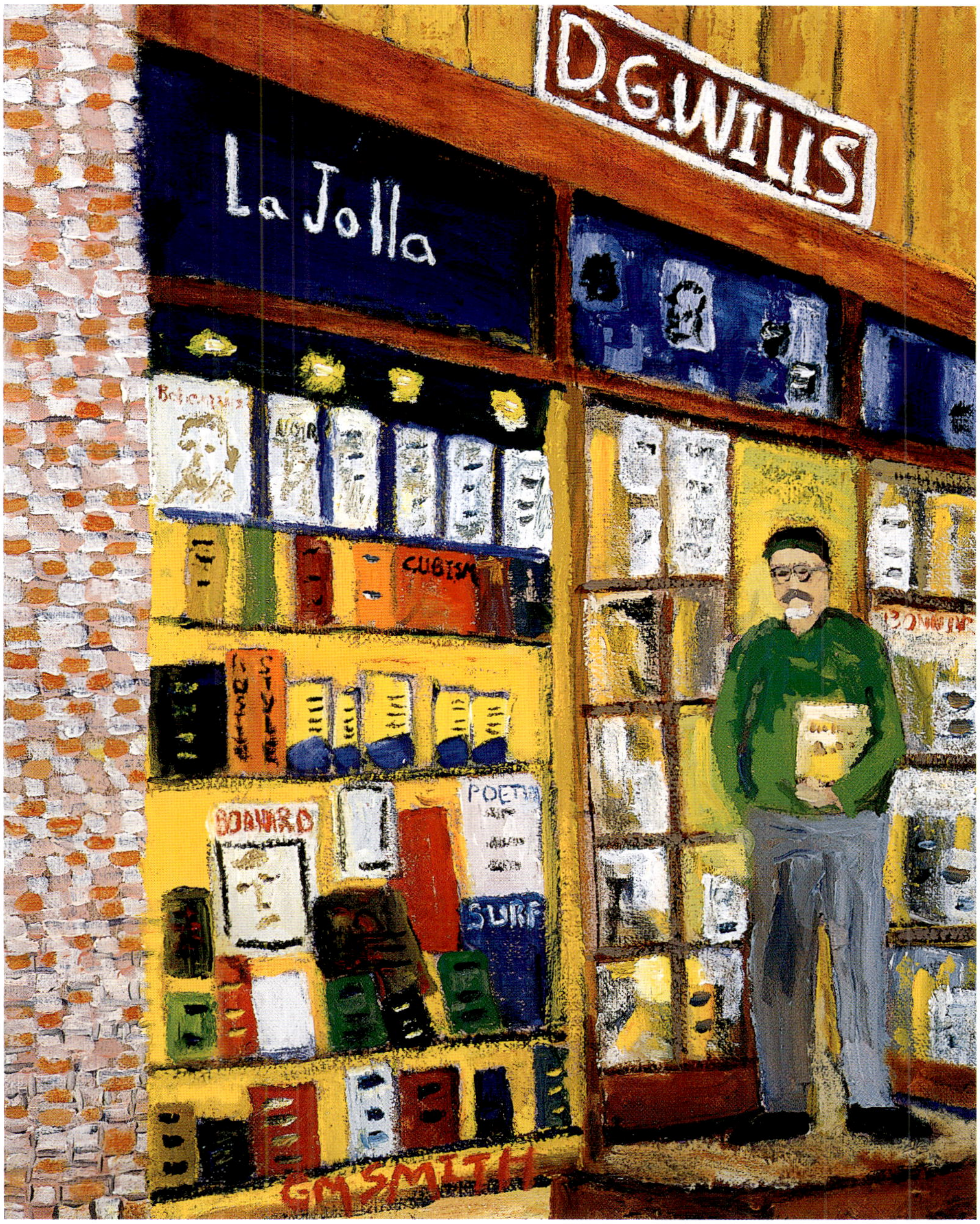

Gibbs M. Smith, La Jolla Bookstore, *2006. Oil on linen, 16" × 20".*

Riverow Bookshop

OWEGO, NEW YORK

John Spencer owns Riverow Bookshop. He created this store and gave it its distinctive color in 1994. He sells new, used, and rare books. The building was built in 1855 and is located in Owego, New York, near Cornell University and close to the Finger Lakes area. The bookshop occupies five floors in this beautiful building and is truly an asset to the community. I was attracted to the store for many reasons, in particular, its wonderful color. Once inside, I found an alluring collection of used books along with old prints and drawings. Every time I visit the store, I enjoy haunting the shelves, looking for hidden treasures.

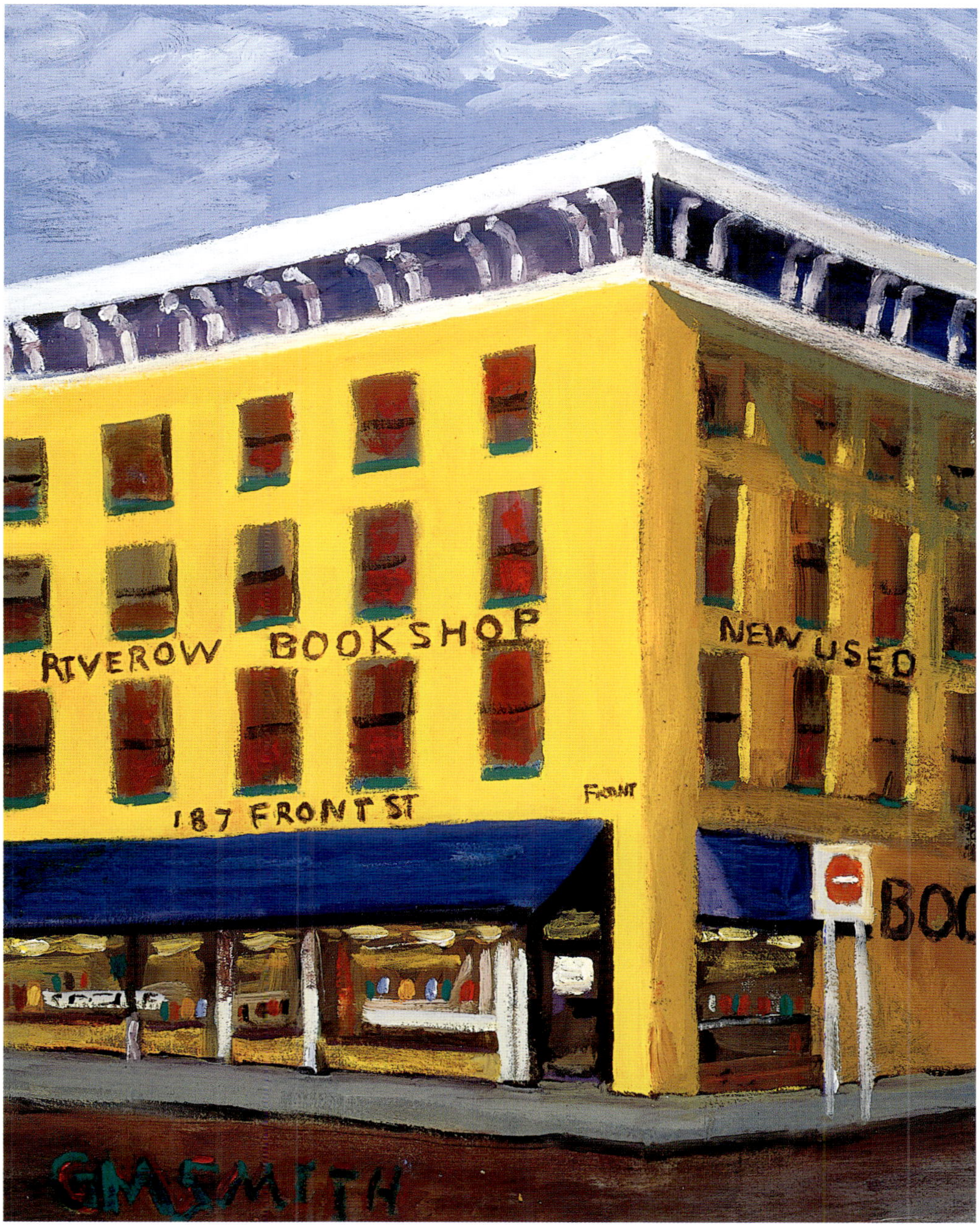

Gibbs M. Smith, Yellow Bookstore, *2005. Oil on linen, 16" × 20".*

Kramerbooks & Afterwords

WASHINGTON, D.C.

Kramerbooks & Afterwords is a Washington institution and one that I am always excited to visit. Located in the Dupont Circle neighborhood and surrounded by universities and research institutions, Kramerbooks is home to a diverse collection of titles, and the store's customers are sophisticated, well read, intelligent, and interesting. This stimulating bookstore is livelier than most thanks to its full-service restaurant, its bar, and its operating hours—"open early to late 7 days a week, all night Friday and Saturday." There is late supper and brunch on weekends and live music Wednesday to Saturday nights.

Kramerbooks is owned and operated by Bill Kramer, who grew up in the book business. His father opened Sidney Kramer Books at the end of World War II and operated it until his death in 1968. Bill took over as manager of Sidney Kramer Books, then opened his own store, Kramerbooks & Afterwords, in 1976.

In 1997, during Kenneth Starr's investigation of the Monica Lewinsky scandal, the store successfully fought a subpoena to provide Starr with a list of the books Lewinsky had purchased there. Bill Kramer told the *Washington Post,* "They are looking for us to hand over information about a specific customer's specific purchases, and that we will not do." The American Booksellers Association, the American Civil Liberties Union, and the American Library Association all stood behind Kramerbooks in their fight.

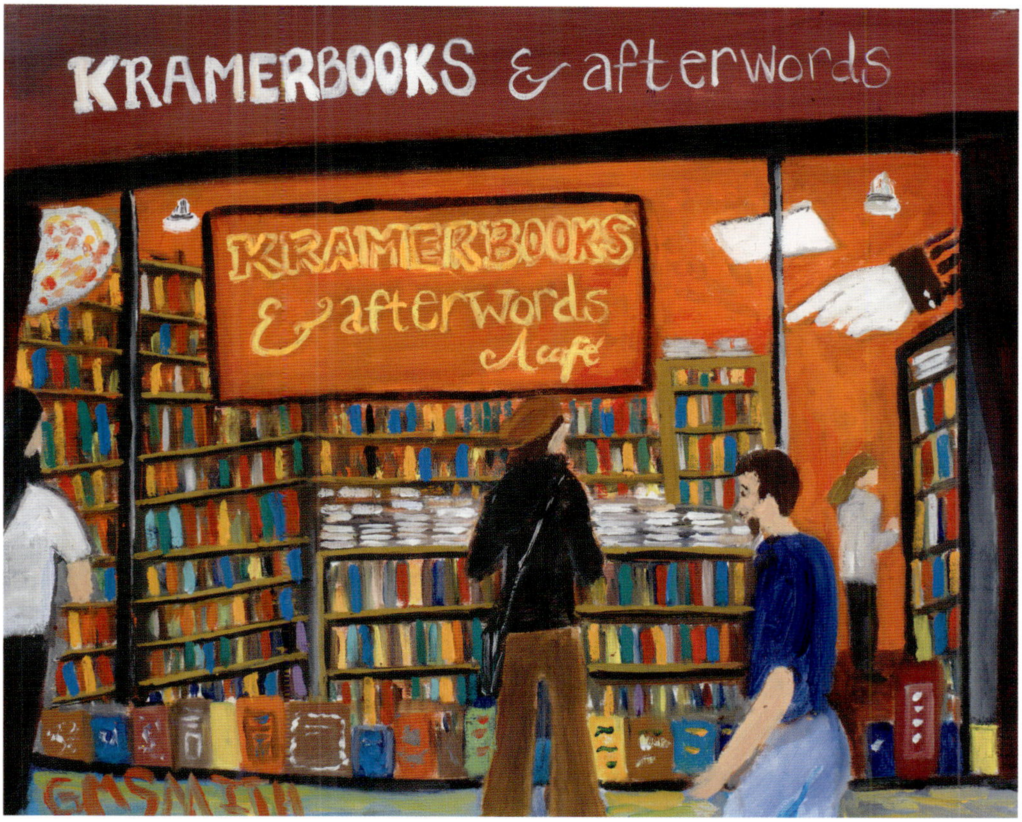

Gibbs M. Smith, Bookstore, Washington, D.C., *2009. Oil on linen, 16" × 20".*

Lenox Hill Bookstore

NEW YORK CITY

Located on upper Lexington Avenue in Manhattan, Lenox Hill Bookstore was owned by Lenny Golay and Ray Sherman, who own The Corner Bookstore on Madison Avenue. Before it closed in 2006, Lenox Hill Bookstore was known for its refined, sophisticated atmosphere. The titles were carefully chosen, and the store boasted an excellent children's section stocked with classics and the best of contemporary fiction. Their selection of art books was excellent.

The painting of this store was created in December 1996: Marcel Duchamp on an easel in front of the store; a solitary pedestrian walking by; a cold December evening; a warm and inviting bookstore. The image captures the feeling I had at that moment.

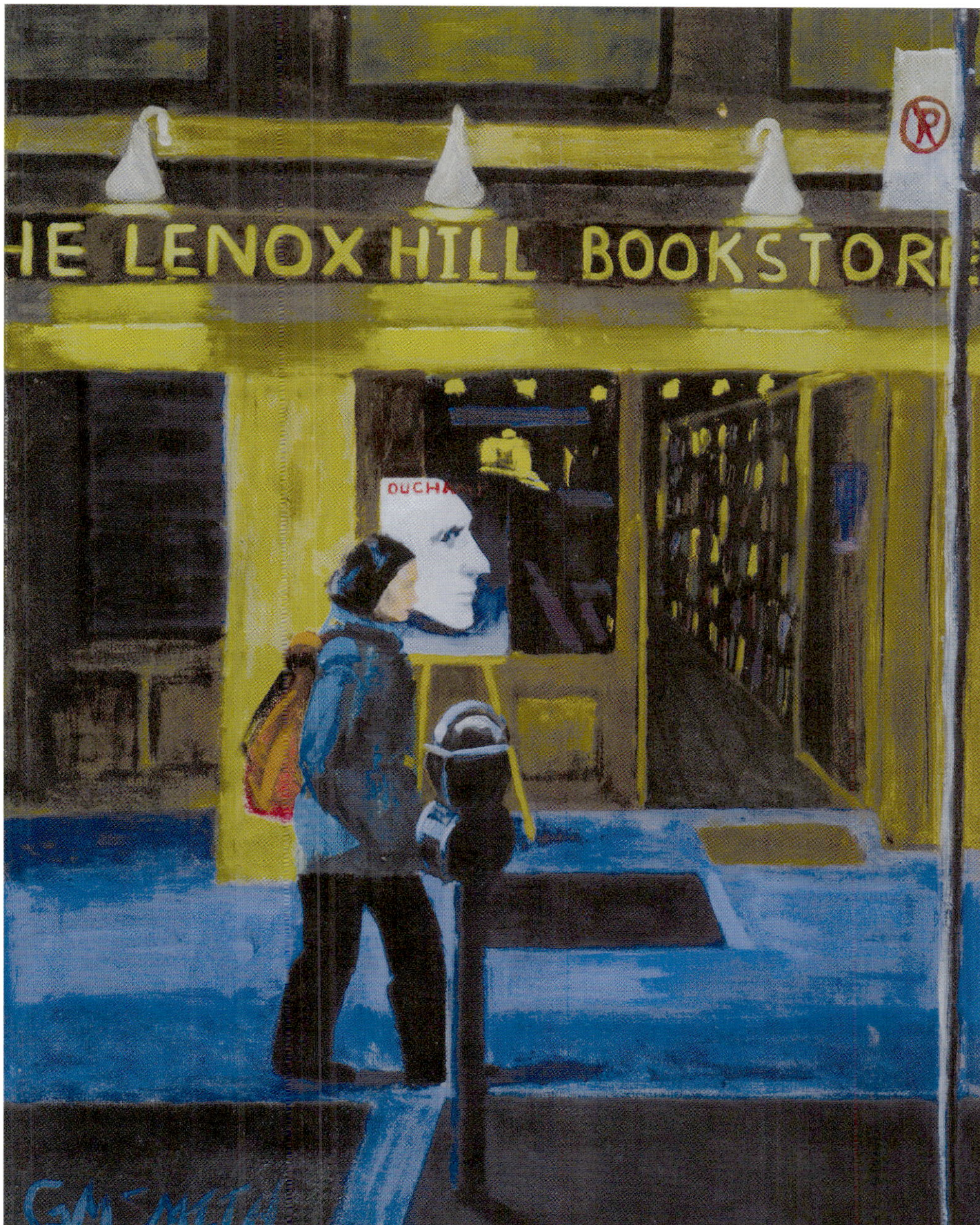

Gibbs M. Smith, Marcel Duchamp and Bookstore, *1996. Oil on linen, 16" × 20".*

Dutton's Beverly Hills Books

BEVERLY HILLS, CALIFORNIA

The Dutton's Beverly Hills bookstore was founded in 2004 by Doug Dutton, who also owned Dutton's in Brentwood. Doug's family is a long-time Southern California bookselling family. His father and mother started Dutton's in the San Fernando Valley, which was later operated by his brother Davis. His sister, Dory, has worked in bookstores throughout the region and is now a sales representative for publishers, including Gibbs Smith, Publisher.

Davis Dutton, Dutton's Books:

It was the autumn of 1960. The country was about to elect a new president, and just about everyone was waiting to see the first-ever televised debate, Nixon vs. Kennedy. Meanwhile, out in California, the Dutton family was about to open a bookstore in Los Angeles.

Or were they? We—my father (Bill) my mother (Thelma) and I—had been discussing and debating this bookstore idea for months. Admittedly we had little experience in the day-to-day mechanics of book retailing, but we did know and love books.

Even as newlyweds in the 1930s, my parents liked nothing more than to browse the old bookstores of Los Angeles: Dawson's, Zeitlin's, Gilbert's with its huge metaphysical collection, and Lou Epstein's famous Pickwick Books on Hollywood Boulevard.

Books had been an important part of our family life, a family that included my siblings Denis, age 16; Douglas, age 12; and kid sister Doris, age 10. Each of these younger Duttons would certainly feel the disruptive effects of a bookstore thrust suddenly into their lives.

And what if we failed? My parents could lose their life savings. So many aspects to be analyzed, so many factors to be weighed. But any lingering doubts were completely dispelled that morning in October

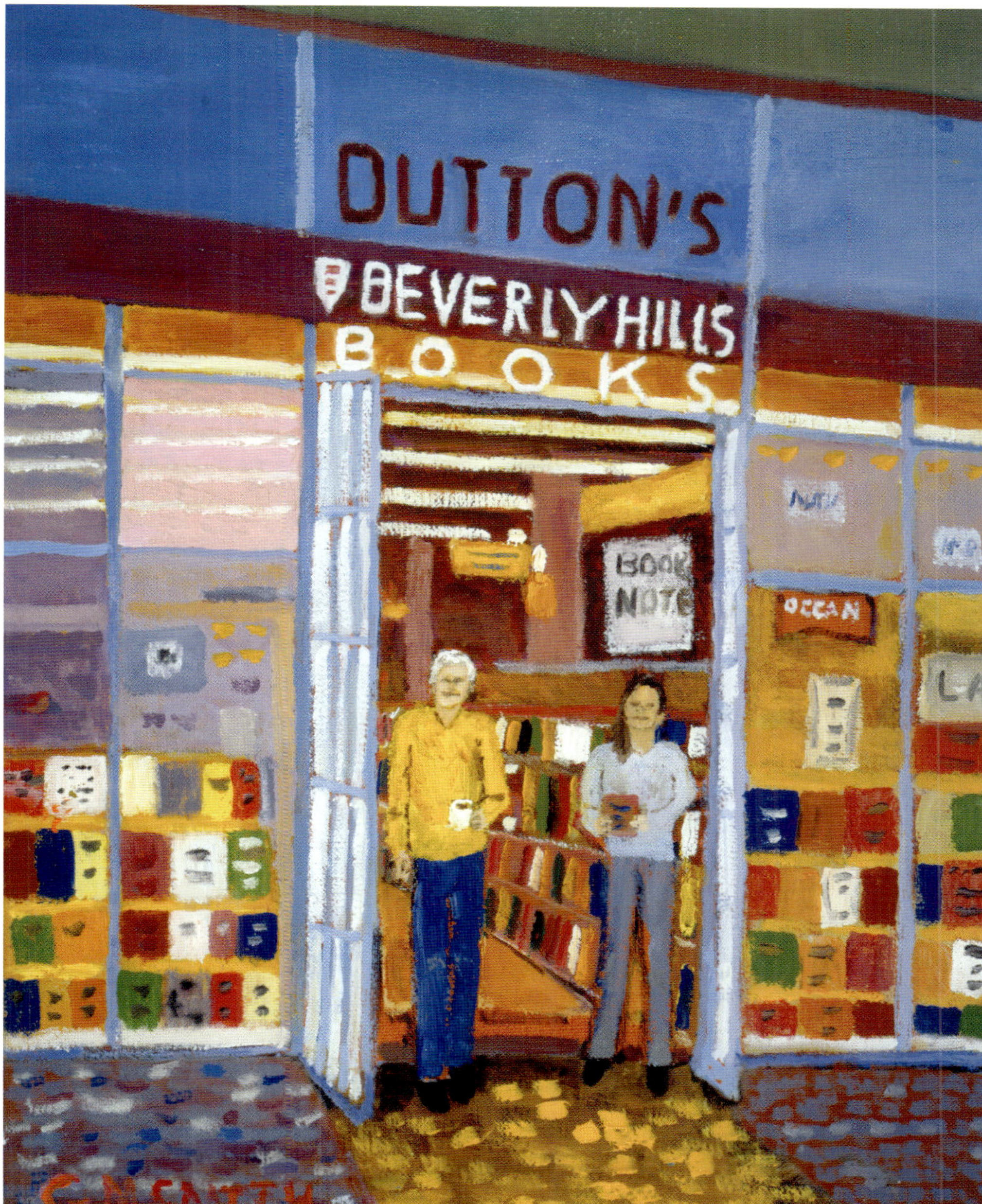

Gibbs M. Smith, Dutton's Beverly Hills, *2007. Oil on linen, 16" × 20".*

1960 when we found the perfect site, a 1,200-square-foot store on Laurel Canyon Boulevard in North Hollywood. The rent was $125 a month. We signed the lease that afternoon.

On January 15, 1961, Dutton's Books opened its doors. It was a quiet, less-than-grand opening. The day's receipts came to $36. We were a success!

In the days and months that followed we did our best to build an inventory, reflecting (and sometimes challenging) the tastes and interests of our clientele. Some categories, like Westerns, just didn't sell. Others, like beat poetry, Cold War spy fiction, and World War II memoirs, did.

We beefed up the reference section, since dictionaries and atlases made great gifts for graduation, birthdays, and bar mitzvahs. It wasn't long before we added used and rare books, giving an intriguing dimension to our stock.

But old books were not easily found. Bill and Thelma made the first of many buying trips abroad, establishing valuable contacts, sources, and friendships that would endure for years.

One day in the early '70s, my sister, Doris, on a lark, brought in a stack of old English prints that she had purchased on London's Portobello Road. The prints were a mix of the comic and the romantic—homely scenes of village life, baleful portraits of kings, queens, and magistrates, and a lively assortment of Shakespearian characters, tragic and triumphant.

The prints sold well—so well that Dory's Print Bin was soon expanded to Dory's Print Room. With Dory herself heading back to England and Wales for more, the store changed its name to Dutton's Books and Prints.

In 1974 we opened a second Dutton's in neighboring Burbank, in the general vicinity of several major studios. The store specialized in film and theater items. We opened another store in 1982 in the food court of downtown Los Angeles' ARCO Plaza. This store became a popular yet peaceful retreat for the office workers from the many floors above.

Shortly thereafter, we opened store #4 in the upscale west side suburb of Brentwood. My brother Doug took charge of this site. Aided by his very capable staff, Doug created a west side literary mecca. The store regularly hosted well-publicized and well-attended author appearances, along with other book events. Dutton's Brentwood became a mandatory stop for any author on a west coast book tour.

Our fifth and final store, also operating under Doug's guidance, was located on Canon Drive in Beverly Hills (shown in Gibbs Smith's painting). It was a charming space, full of good literature, classic and modern, and beautiful volumes on art, architecture, and travel. The store also had a well-stocked music section and a cute café.

A full history of bookselling in Los Angeles has yet to be written. When it is, it will prove to be a colorful tale, a vivid chronicle of dedicated dealers, grateful readers, collectors both major and minor, dilettantes, scholars, and librarians, along with a smattering of scoundrels, con artists, and a few downright crooks.

What place Dutton's will occupy in this procession remains to be seen. I'm heartened by a recent blog entry, written by Paul L. Martin, a teacher and former customer. I quote, in part:

"My heart will always belong to Dutton's in North Hollywood. . . . I would prowl its musty dusty aisles and find a number of reasonably priced gems to stock my growing shelves at home.

"Dutton's is where I purchased my complete Pepys' Diary. . . . Some philosopher once said that we die twice—once physically, and once when everyone who remembered us dies.

"Well, Dutton's lives on. I remember. My bookshelves are loaded with Dutton books. I will keep the memory alive."

The Elliott Bay Book Company

SEATTLE, WASHINGTON

The Elliott Bay Book Company was originally founded in 1973 by Walter Carr, with Peter Aaron taking over ownership in 1998. Located in historic Pioneer Square in Seattle, Washington, the bookstore resides in the historic Globe Building, which is still standing despite having gone through three fires and two earthquakes in its long, colorful life. Originally designed in 1890 as an office building with commercial space on the main floor, the Globe turned into the Windsor Hotel in 1889 to meet the flood of immigrants that were arriving in the city. The hotel remained in business until the late 1960s, along with a saloon that operated from 1891 to 1970. Other occupants of the building during its long history include the Alaska Gold Standard Mining Co., the Seattle Quilt Company, and a woman's barbershop rumored to have been a front for prostitution.

During the time that the Elliott Bay Book Company has occupied the Globe Building it has grown and expanded downstairs where, in 1979, the Elliott Bay Café opened.

Hosting hundreds of author appearances each year, Peter Aaron and his staff at Elliott Bay are not shy when it comes to their passion for the books they sell.

I always love visiting the store, both for its wide selection of books and for the neighborhood. Around the corner from Elliott Bay is the Alaskan Gold Rush Museum and, when I am there, I often think of my grandfather, who traveled from Seattle to be part of the Alaskan gold rush. (He was successful.)

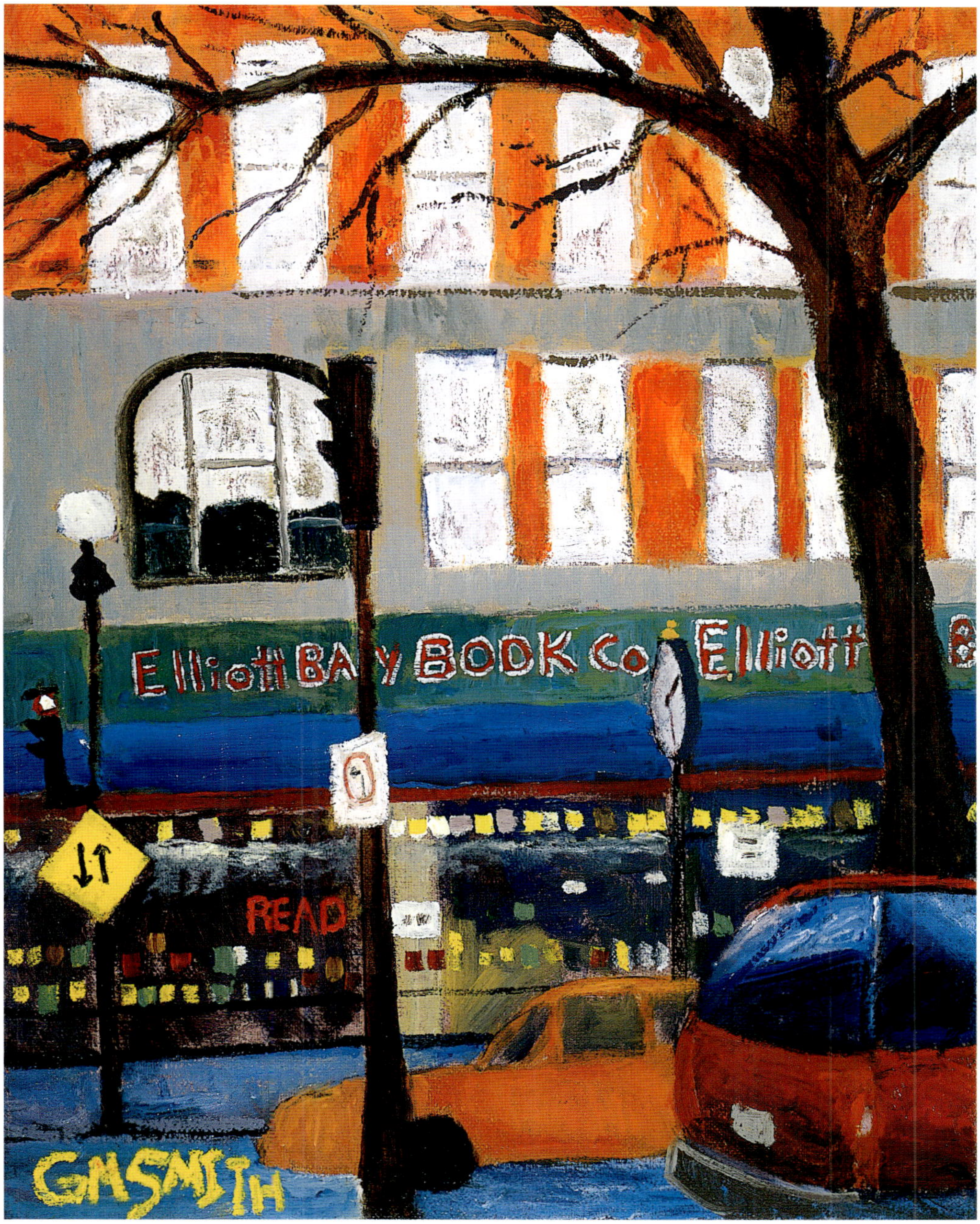

Gibbs M. Smith, Bookstore, Seattle, *2006. Oil on linen, 16" × 20".*

Garcia Street Books

SANTA FE, NEW MEXICO

by Edward Borins, co-owner of Garcia Street Books

My wife, Eva, and I began our bookselling careers in Toronto, in 1973, when we opened David Mivirsh Books on Art, the first art bookstore in Canada. In 1979 we opened our own bookstore, Edward's Books and Art, which grew into one of Canada's largest independent chains. In 1997 we closed our stores and moved to Santa Fe, where we thought we would enjoy our retirement.

But bookselling and retirement do not agree, so in May of 2000 we purchased the store across the road from where we lived and continued Garcia Street Books, which was established in 1991. We were back in the saddle again.

Some of our friends and family questioned our sanity in returning to what was perceived as a dying business, but, after almost ten years as booksellers in Santa Fe, our investment has yielded many dividends, both financial and personal.

"We are having more fun than ever with our little 'retirement bookstore.' Santa Fe is one of the few cities in North America where we would want to own a bookstore, and our customers are intelligent, well read, and extremely supportive. Where else could two Nobel Laureates walk in on the same day?

The art of the bookstore involves the basics that all successful booksellers know, but in these times it takes more than just the basics to thrive. We do exhibitions of rare artists' books, made by the great masters such as Picasso and Matisse. We also average seven events a month involving local and celebrity authors, such as Jane Fonda, Maureen Dowd, Shirley MacLaine, and Valerie Plame.

In all the years of staging these events we had only one mishap when a flustered Stuart Woods arrived an hour late wearing his central time watch as we were closing our doors.

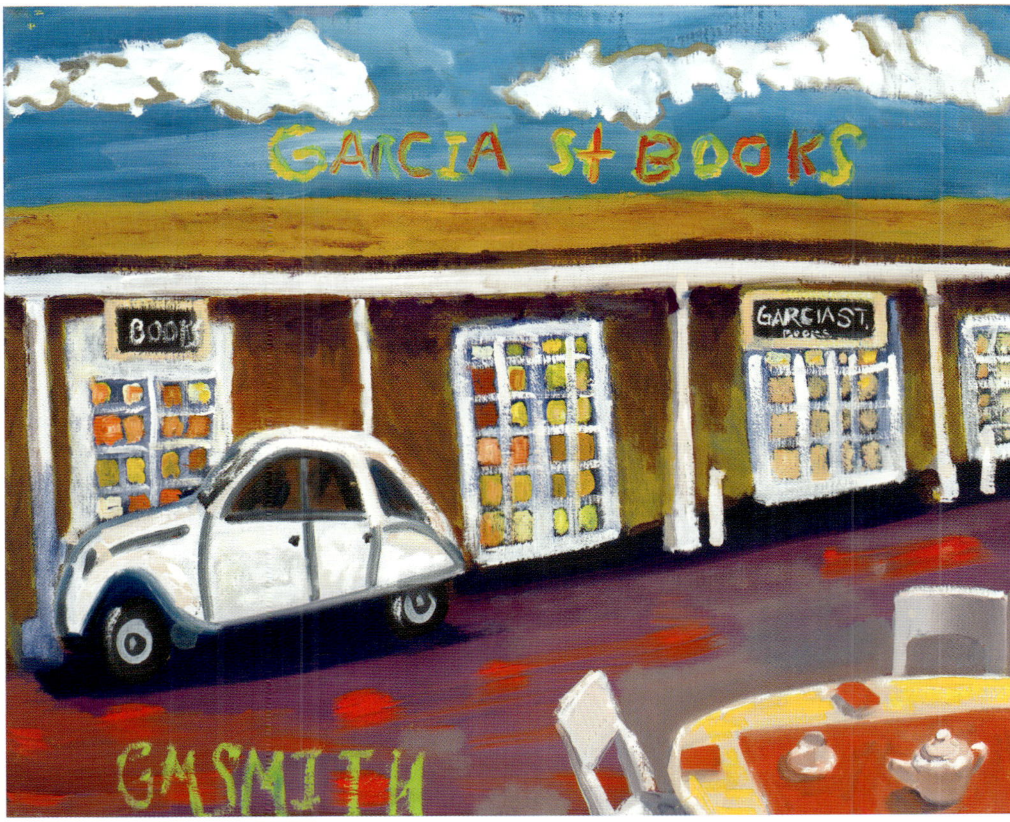

Gibbs M. Smith, Garcia Street, Santa Fe, *2009. Oil on linen, 16" × 20".*

Gotham Book Mart

NEW YORK CITY

When Gotham Book Mart closed its doors in 2007, New York lost a significant cultural landmark. Located in the midst of New York's diamond district, Gotham was known as a literary sanctuary that attracted writers and artists and promoted thought-provoking literature. Gotham was opened in 1920 by Frances Steloff, a passionate book lover and businesswoman who continued to work in and nurture the store even after selling it to Andreas Brown in 1967. The store was managed by my friend Philip Lyman, who grew up in southern Utah.

The bookstore was frequented over the years by such writers and other artists as Theodore Dreiser, Arthur Miller, John Updike, J. D. Salinger, George and Ira Gershwin, Charlie Chaplin, Alexander Calder, Woody Allen, Saul Bellow, and Katharine Hepburn. Its walls held memorabilia of readings from such poets as Dylan Thomas and W. H. Auden. The artist Edward Gorey, a good friend of Andreas Brown's, launched his career at Gotham when Brown exhibited and sold his works where Gorey was still unknown. Customers loved the store for its out-of-the-ordinary selection and its eccentric atmosphere.

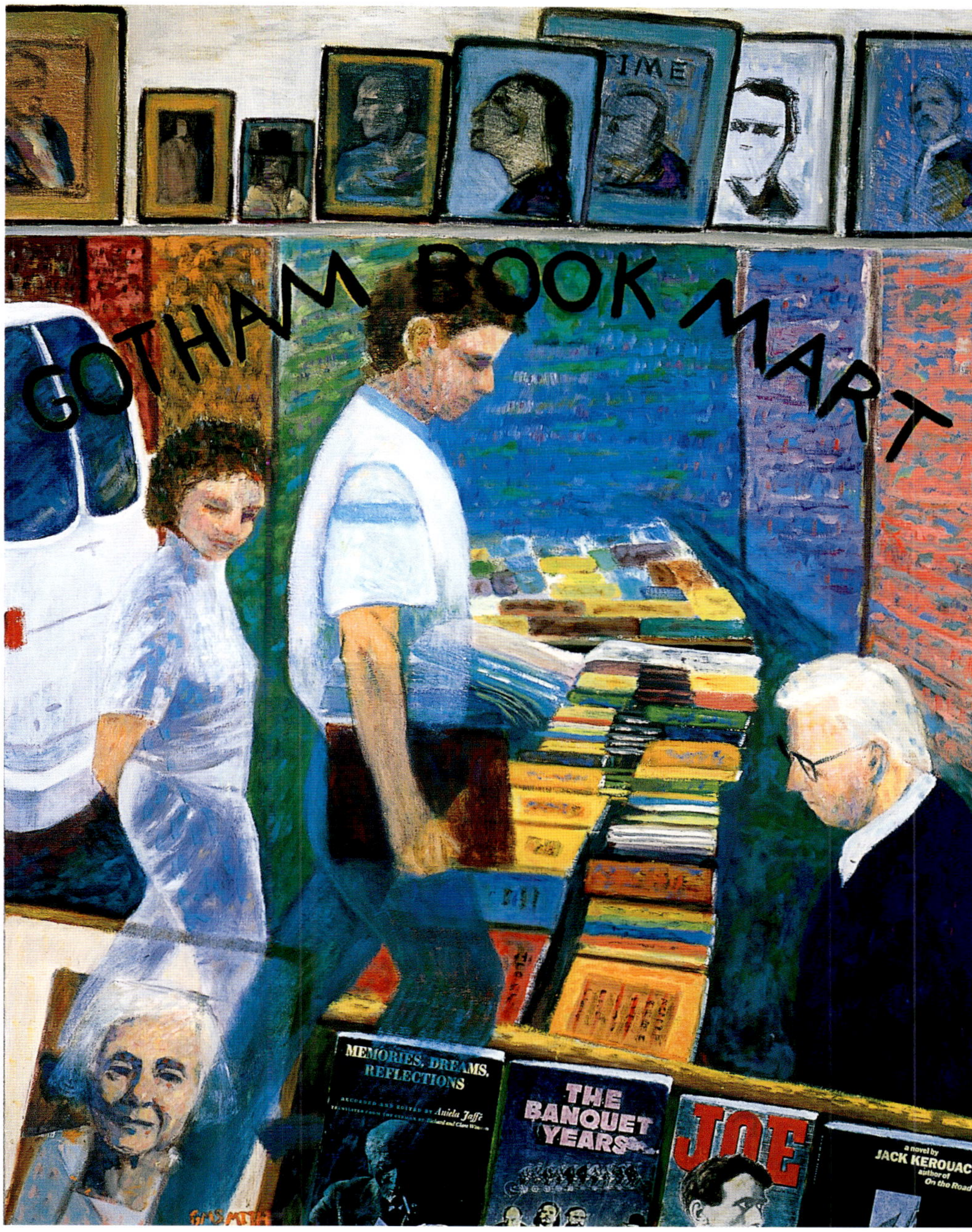

Gibbs M. Smith, Frances's Bookstore, New York, *1990. Oil on canvas, 16" × 20".*

Green Apple Books

SAN FRANCISCO, CALIFORNIA

Located on Clement Street in San Francisco, Green Apple Books has been owned and operated by Kevin Ryan, Pete Mulvihill, and Kevin Hunsanger since 1999; it was originally opened in 1967 by Richard Savoy. Green Apple has three floors of crooked aisles, secret alcoves, and hidden stairways—a perfect place for book lovers to lose themselves or find something unexpected. With the store's very knowledgeable and friendly staff, you can often find titles at Green Apple that you won't find in other bookstores.

Kevin Ryan, co-owner of Green Apple Books:

The art of bookselling to me means embracing that word "independent," being our own store and not necessarily everybody's store. Some people don't like Green Apple because they think it's a little messy or it's just not their cup of tea. But the people that like it like it ferociously. Our customers want a place that's their own, and they're more loyal as a result than they would be if they could get the same experience shopping anywhere else.

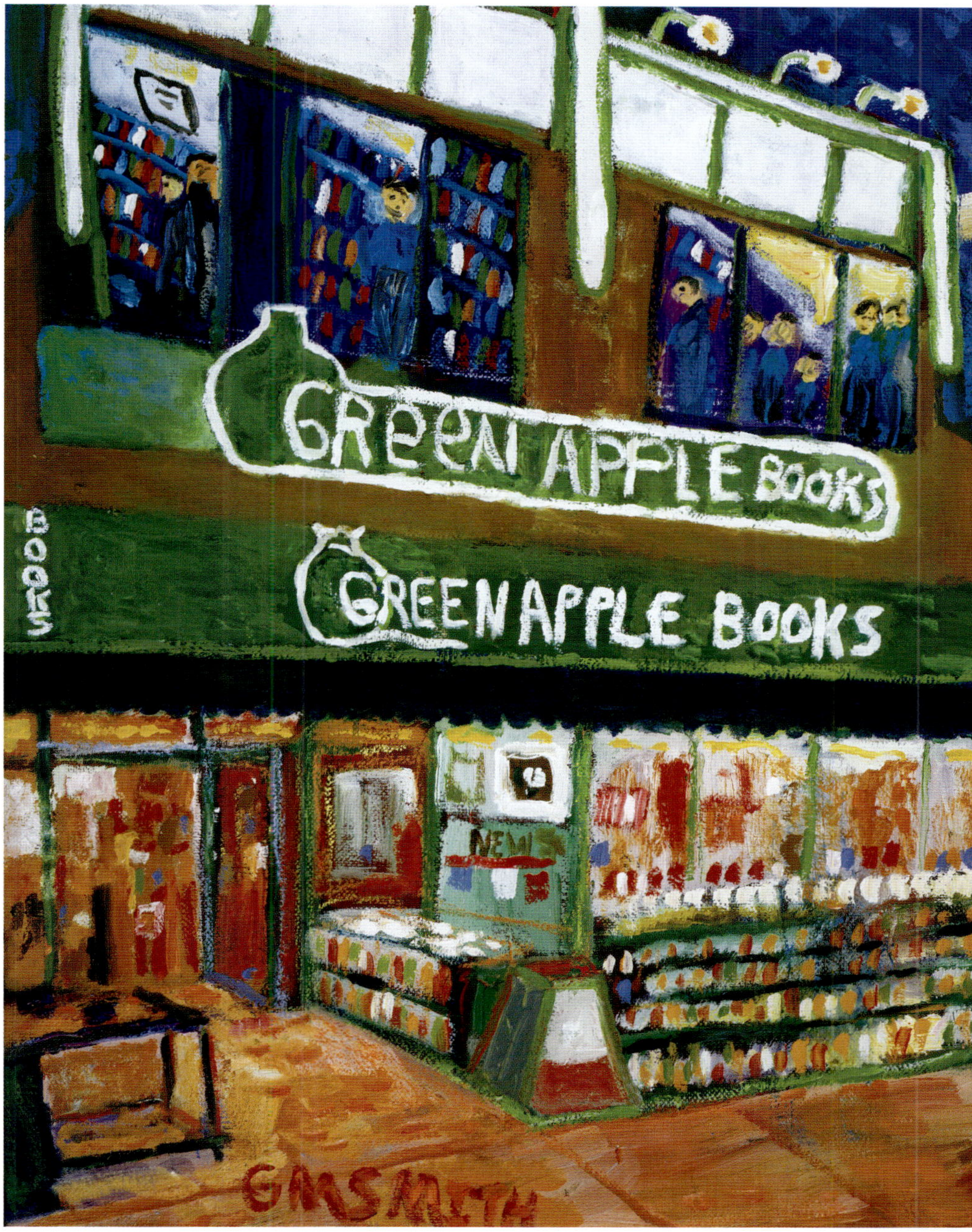

Gibbs M. Smith, Green Apple, *2008. Oil on linen, 16" × 20".*

Hennessey + Ingalls

SANTA MONICA, CALIFORNIA

Hennessey + Ingalls is one of the greatest bookstores in the country dealing with visual arts. Founded in 1963 and still family owned, the store has followed the trends of California design from the days of John Entenza's *Art & Architecture* magazine and the Case Study House Program to today's cutting-edge architecture and design. After almost twenty years in their Morphosis-designed building on Santa Monica's Third Street Promenade, Hennessey + Ingalls moved to new quarters around the corner on Wilshire Boulevard. In the 1960s as a graduate student, I spent many enjoyable hours in Hennessey + Ingalls with my mentor, architectural historian David Gebhard.

The love of learning, the sequestered nooks,
And all the sweet serenity of books.

—Henry Wadsworth Longfellow

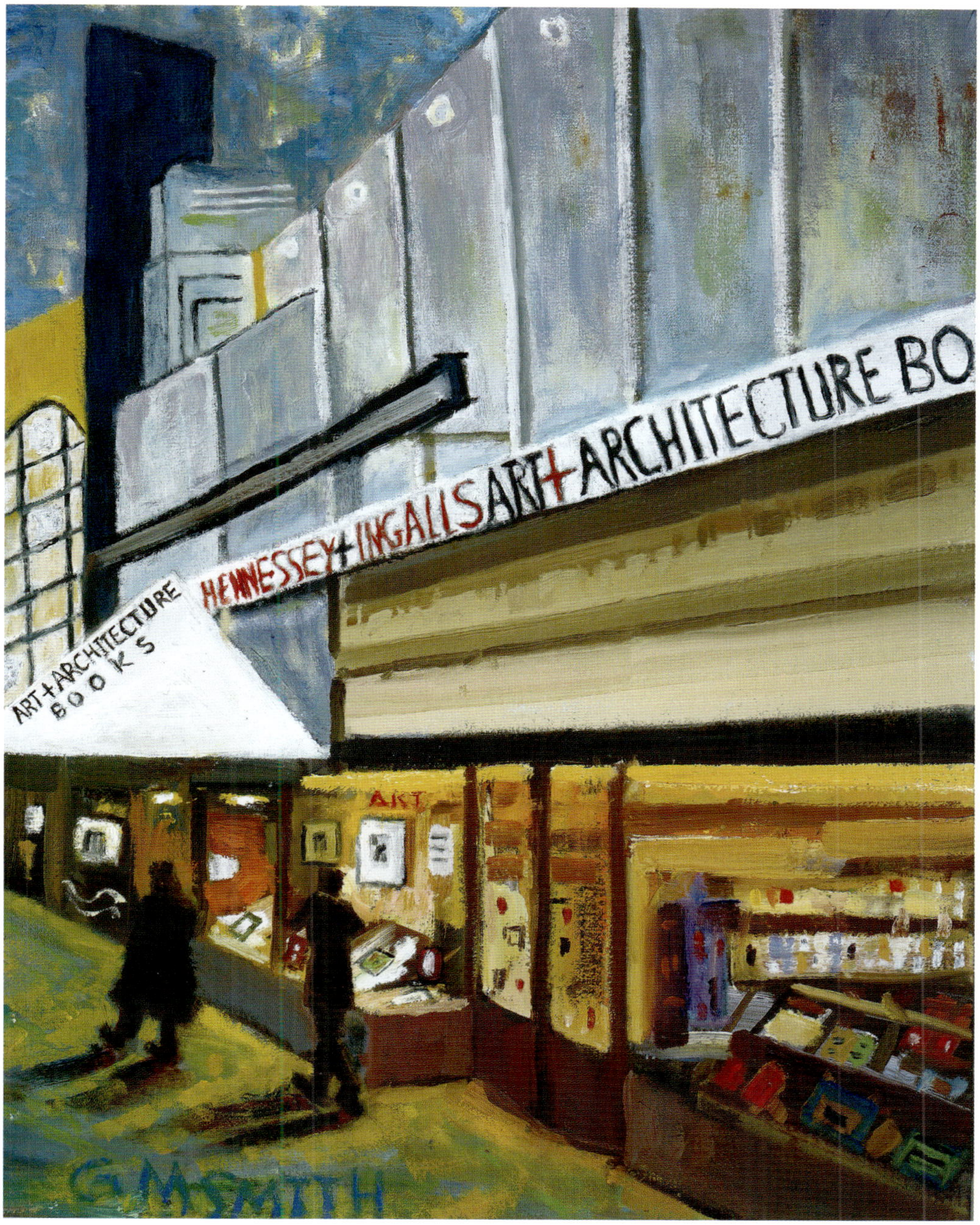

Gibbs M. Smith, Hennessey & Ingalls, *2003. Oil on linen, 16" × 20".*

Jay's Book Stall

PITTSBURGH, PENNSYLVANIA

Founded and operated by Jay Dantry, Jay's Book Stall was in business in Pittsburgh in the heart of Pittsburgh's university, medical, and museum community for forty-nine years. The venerable shop was wall-to-wall, floor-to-ceiling books, and nearly five hundred photographs of Jay with visiting writers were featured along display panels, on counters, and in alcoves. The pictures included such writers as Kurt Vonnegut, John Updike, Stephen King, Erica Jong, and Pulitzer Prize–winning novelist and former Book Stall clerk Michael Chabon. Jay also remembers the distinguished Broadway actors who, as students, used to spend hours perched on ladders in the drama section reading playbooks.

At the age of seventy-nine Jay decided to retire and close his shop, disappointing the many die-hard customers who came to rely on him. Jay helped his customers find little-known literary gems and connected readers with authors through the hundreds of book signings and readings he held over the years. Jay leaves behind a legacy of a passion for books and a love of sharing that passion with everyone who walked through his doors.

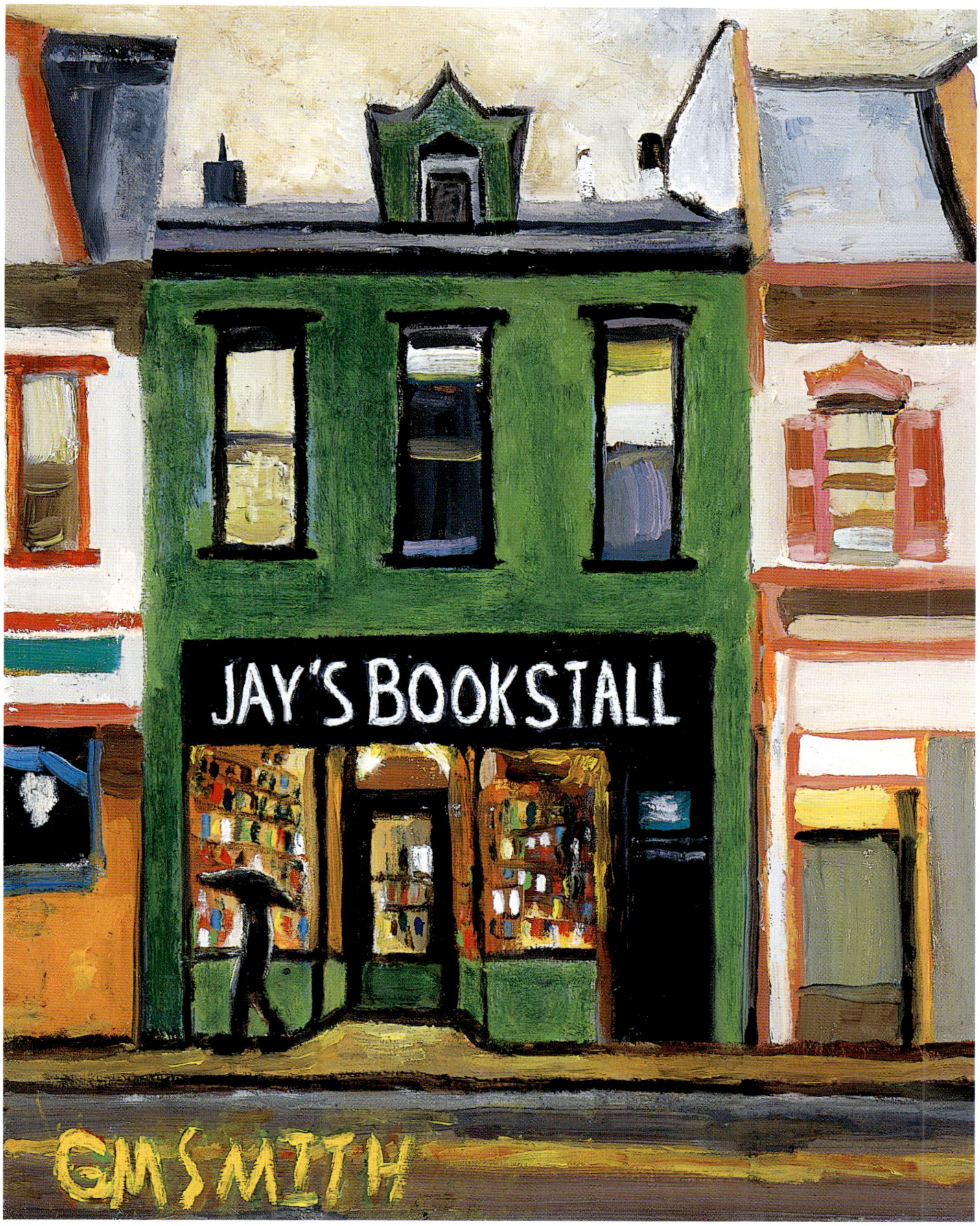

Gibbs M. Smith, Jay's Book Stall, *2004. Oil on linen, 16" × 20".*

El Ateneo Grand Splendid

BUENOS AIRES, ARGENTINA

This store has perhaps the most unusual location—in a former opera house in Buenos Aires. Originally built by Argentine entrepreneur Max Glücksmann, the Teatro Grand Splendid opened in May 1919 as a live theatre with a seating capacity of 1,050. In 1924, a radio station, LR4 Radio Splendid, began broadcasting from the upper floor of the building, where Glücksmann's recording studios were also located. Many great tango artists of the day made their first recordings there, and tango contests were also held annually in the theatre. It was later converted into a cinema in the late 1920s, operating until its closure in the late 1990s. Declared a historic landmark, El Ateneo has served as possibly the most luxurious bookshop in the world since 2000, with its balcony and domed ceiling with paintings by Italian artist Nazarino Orlandi, cherubs, marble columns, and elaborate sconces. You can even enjoy a cup of coffee in the stylish café, which is located on the former stage.

On the ground floor you will find in the space once occupied by armchairs, rows upon rows of bookshelves holding a vast selection of art, architecture, cinema, cookbooks, novels, dictionaries, health, and business books, most in Spanish; however, you can also find an interesting selection of English books as well.

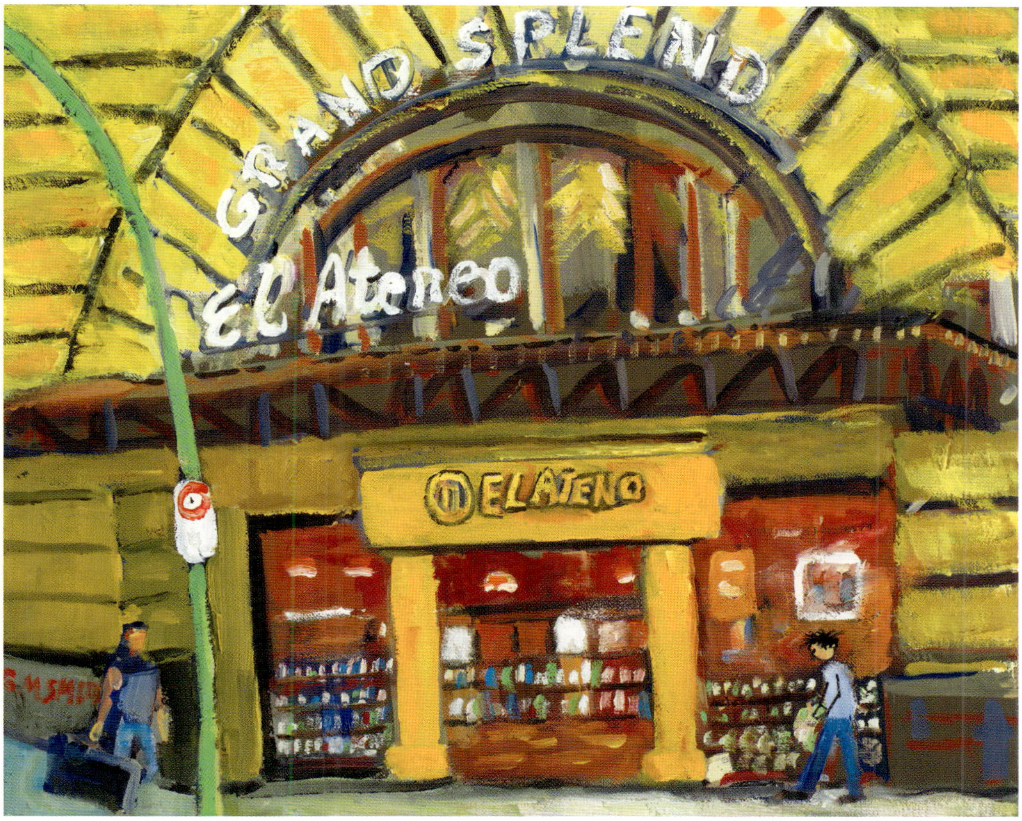

Gibbs M. Smith, Bookstore, Buenos Aires, *2009. Oil on linen, 16" × 20".*

Ken Sanders Rare Books

SALT LAKE CITY, UTAH

by Ken Sanders, owner of Ken Sanders Rare Books

In some manner or another, I have been involved in the world of books virtually all my life.

From the beginning, the word was there, and I read it, revered it, and devoured it. Later, my childhood appetite for reading broadened into a desire to collect books, as well as read them. I also came to love them as physical objects—I began to appreciate their bindings and design, their illustrations and typography, as well as their content. I looked at them, fondled them, and inhaled them. If there was a God, his name was Biblio.

In the last fifty years, my roles in the book world have included reader, collector, new bookseller, antiquarian book dealer, publisher, editor, occasional writer, and always champion of the printed world in all its myriad manifestations. In these early years of the twenty-first century, there has been an awful lot of talk about 'the death of the book.' What is being forgotten in this dialogue is that devotees of the book have always been on the margins of society—in modern society, book lovers are about as mainstream as druids. Whether two thousand years ago in the great lost library of Alexandria, half a millennium ago in Gutenberg's time, or at any time and place since human beings first articulated their thoughts on clay, stone, and papyrus, those of us involved in these matters have always lived in some far distant corner of the universe.

There has been a great upheaval in information distribution in the last few decades that is accelerating as we speak. No one now living on the planet knows where it will end up. Google, Wikipedia, the World Wide Web, Kindle, e-books, print on demand, and the next new thing threaten to extinguish the old-fashioned book. Perhaps. I think not: the transformation will continue. The value of books transcends the informational, and while some of us in the book world will become extinct, the rest of us will always be here, doing what we have always done: loving books, keeping Biblio alive in the world.

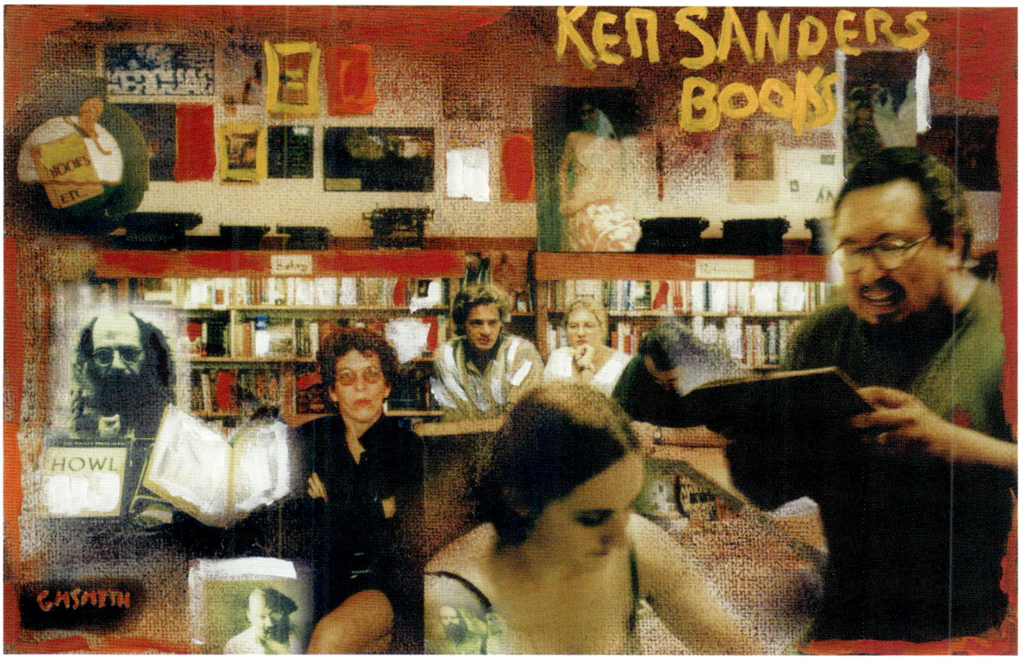

Gibbs M. Smith, Ken Sanders Books, *2005. Mixed media, 16″ × 20″.*

Prairie Avenue Bookshop

CHICAGO, ILLINOIS

Downtown Chicago is home to one of the largest and best bookstores on architecture and design. Prairie Avenue Bookshop was opened by Marilyn and Wilbert Hasbrouck. The Hasbroucks had founded the Prairie School Press in 1961 in order to publish books about Prairie School architecture. Following that, they founded the *Prairie School Review,* a quarterly journal that served as a forum for discussion about the architectural style. The Hasbroucks began selling books to subsidize publication of the journal, and this led to the opening of Prairie Avenue Bookshop in 1974.

Since then, the shop has become a mecca for all things architecture and design. Just visiting the store is an architectural treat. Wilbert Hasbrouck is an architect himself, and when the store moved to its new quarters on Wabash Avenue, Wilbert designed a space with Prairie School and Chicago School influences. The store is even decorated with furniture by Frank Lloyd Wright, Mies van der Rohe, Le Corbusier, and others. The shop's collection of titles is impressive and intelligent. I am always amazed at their inventory, and as a lover of architecture and art, I appreciate the significance of a store dedicated to celebrating these important fields.

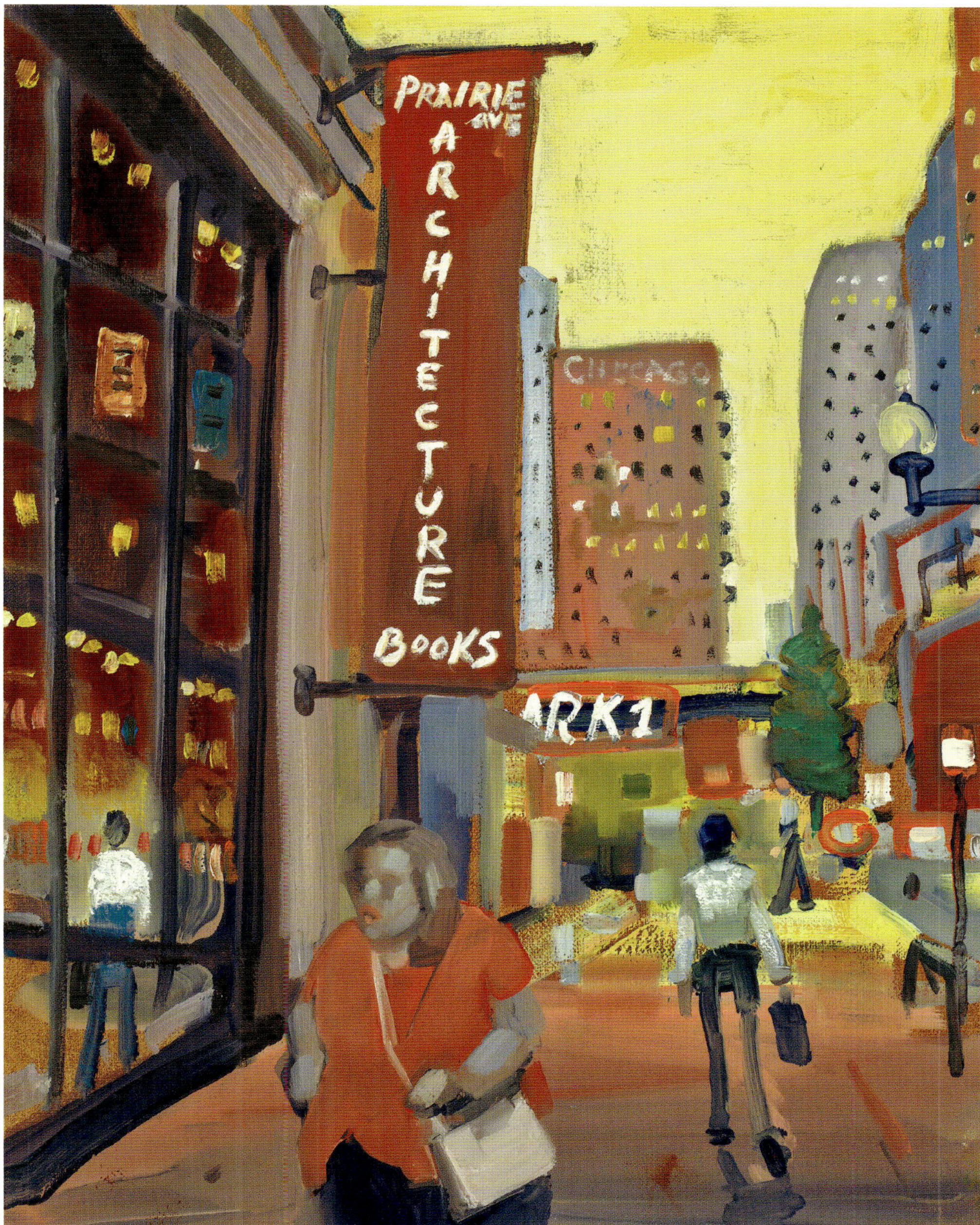

Gibbs M. Smith, Prairie Avenue Books, *2009. Oil on linen, 16" × 20".*

Kepler's Books

MENLO PARK, CALIFORNIA

by Clark Kepler, president, CEO, and chairman of Kepler's Books

In 1955 my father, Roy Kepler, helped usher in the paperback revolution by opening one of the first paperback bookstores in Northern California. Dad's goal was to achieve a 'right livelihood,' to provide for his family, and to serve the community by making available the full range of humankind's ideas.

He believed that booksellers fill a very important role in our democracy, that what we sell has far greater impact on our community than mere merchandise. Books capture the greatest ideas of humankind and a bookseller's role is to provide a full range of these ideas, 'good' and 'bad,' left and right, whatever interests an inquiring mind. In a democracy, people must make choices. They cannot do that unless they know what their choices are.

While the world has changed since 1955, Kepler's remains dedicated, in this generation as in the last, to be an informed provider of information in our rapidly developing age of information, preserving free speech and the right to free inquiry. We are an independent bookstore that is committed to selling great books, the free exchange of intellectual ideas, and making a significant and lasting contribution to the community.

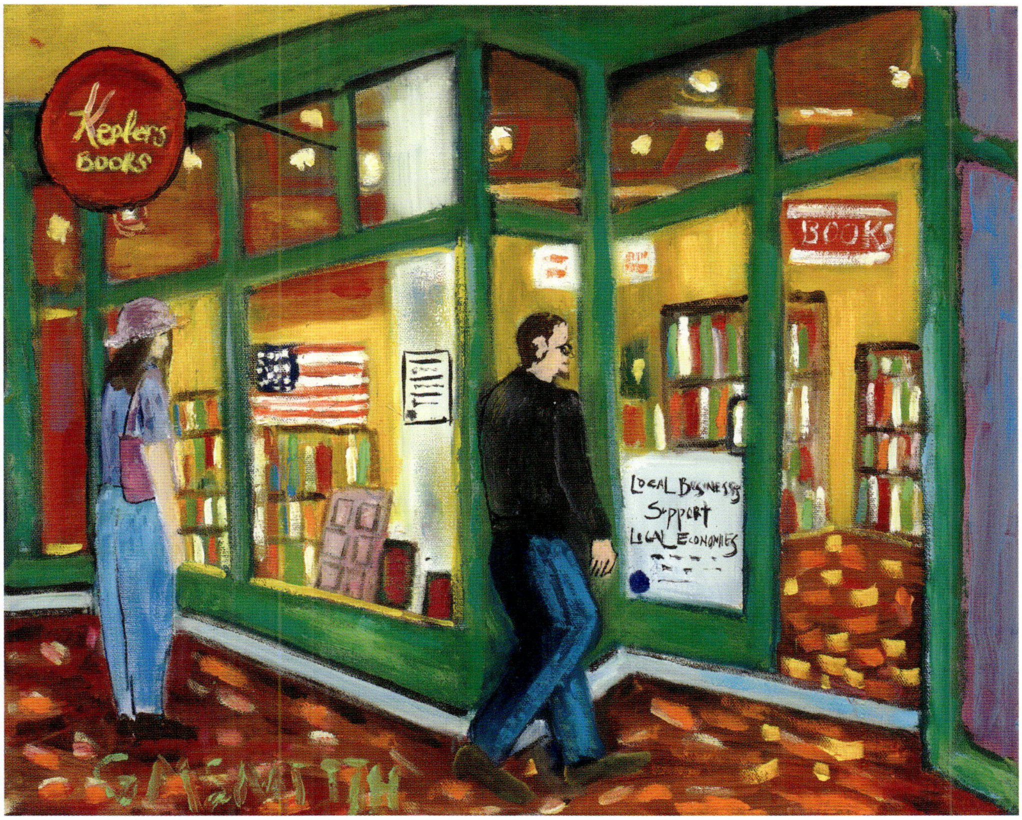

Gibbs M. Smith, Kepler's*, 2009. Oil on linen, 16" × 20".*

Madison Avenue Bookshop

NEW YORK CITY

Madison Avenue Bookshop was located in the heart of the Upper East Side's shopping area at 833 Madison Avenue. With its elegant tailored façade, the shop long served its distinguished neighborhood. It was a place I always enjoyed visiting and where I discovered many of my favorite books. I did a sketch of this store in December of 2001, and the flag was placed in the window marking the tragedy of 9/11.

The store was opened in 1973 by Arthur Lehman Loeb, who ended up giving the store and the building to Perry Haberman, a longtime employee who had become the store's manager. In 2003, Haberman made the difficult decision to close the store. Its many longtime customers felt the loss. Madison Avenue Bookshop was the kind of store where the salespeople knew you by name, would select titles specifically for you, and would order and hand deliver books to your residence. The Upper East Side lost a neighborhood treasure when Madison Avenue Bookshop closed its doors.

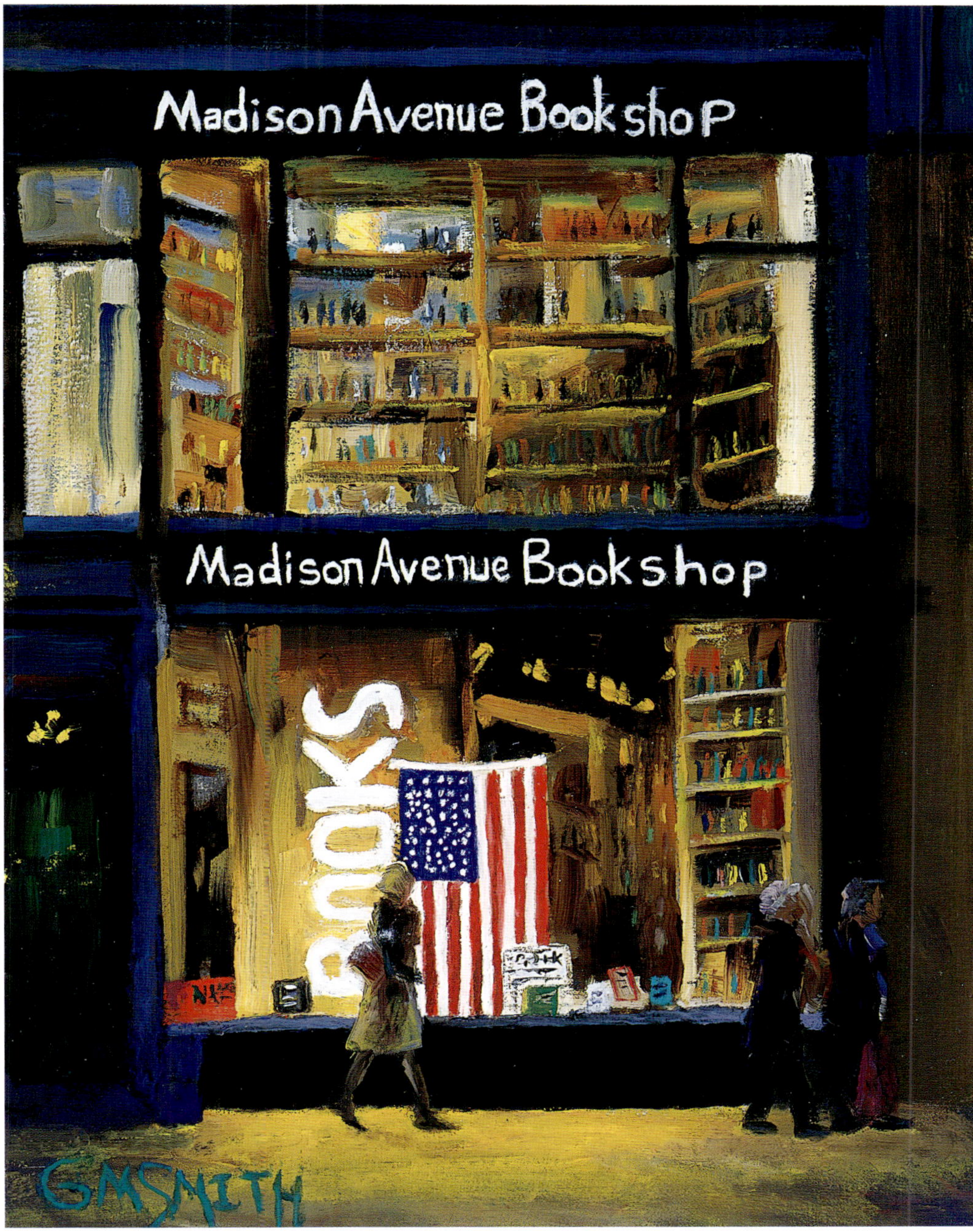

Gibbs M. Smith, Madison Avenue Bookshop, 2002. *Oil on linen, 16" × 20".*

Maria's Bookshop

DURANGO, COLORADO

Located on Main Avenue in Durango, Colorado, Maria's Bookshop is a local treasure that is dedicated to its community. The warm, inviting store is decorated with works from local artists. Local authors hold readings and signings there. Skis, sleds, and snowshoes on the walls emphasize the regional flavor of this store, which proudly celebrates the history, culture, and landscape of Durango and the entire Southwest. In fact, Maria's Bookshop isn't named for an owner or founder of the store; rather, it's a tribute to Maria Martinez, the famous potter from the San Ildefonso Pueblo, which is located in neighboring New Mexico.

It seems that everyone who works at Maria's is an outdoor enthusiast who loves the mountain country as well as books. The store was founded by a river rafter, and the current owners and staff are skiers, hikers, and cyclers. It's not a surprise, then, that owners Andrea Avantaggio and Peter Schertz are committed to the environment. The company uses wind power, encourages its employees to bike to work, provides free trolley tokens to its customers, uses green cleaning products, and even has beehives on its roof. The store supports the community by carrying and promoting books by local authors, as well as by selling locally made products such as jewelry, journals, and greeting cards. The citizens of Durango respond by making Maria's a successful business year after year.

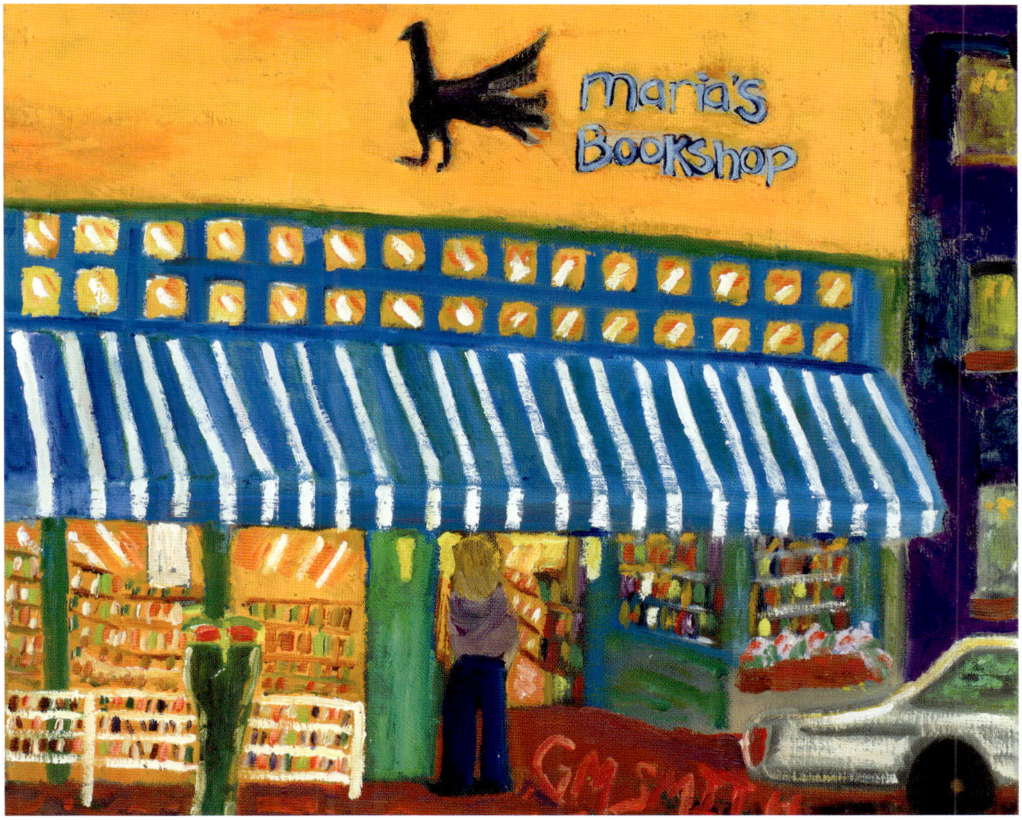

Gibbs M. Smith, Maria's, 2009. *Oil on linen, 16" × 20".*

Mrs. Dalloway's Literary & Garden Arts

BERKELEY, CALIFORNIA

Owned by Ann Leyhe and Marion Abbott Bundy and founded in 2004, this store is managed with much style and taste. The name of the store comes from a book by Virginia Woolf of the same title, which was written the same year the store's building was constructed. A unique feature of Mrs. Dalloway's is the mannequin that takes center stage in the front window, stylishly dressed for each new season. In addition to fiction, children's literature, biography, politics, and history, Mrs. Dalloway's has a wonderful assortment of gardening books, as well as plants, flowerpots and vases, and an extensive collection of gardening magazines.

Tough choices face the biblioholic at every step of the way—like choosing between reading and eating, between buying new clothes and buying books, between a reasonable lifestyle and one of penurious but masochistic happiness lived out in the wallow of excess.

—Tom Raabe,
Biblioholism: The Literary Addiction

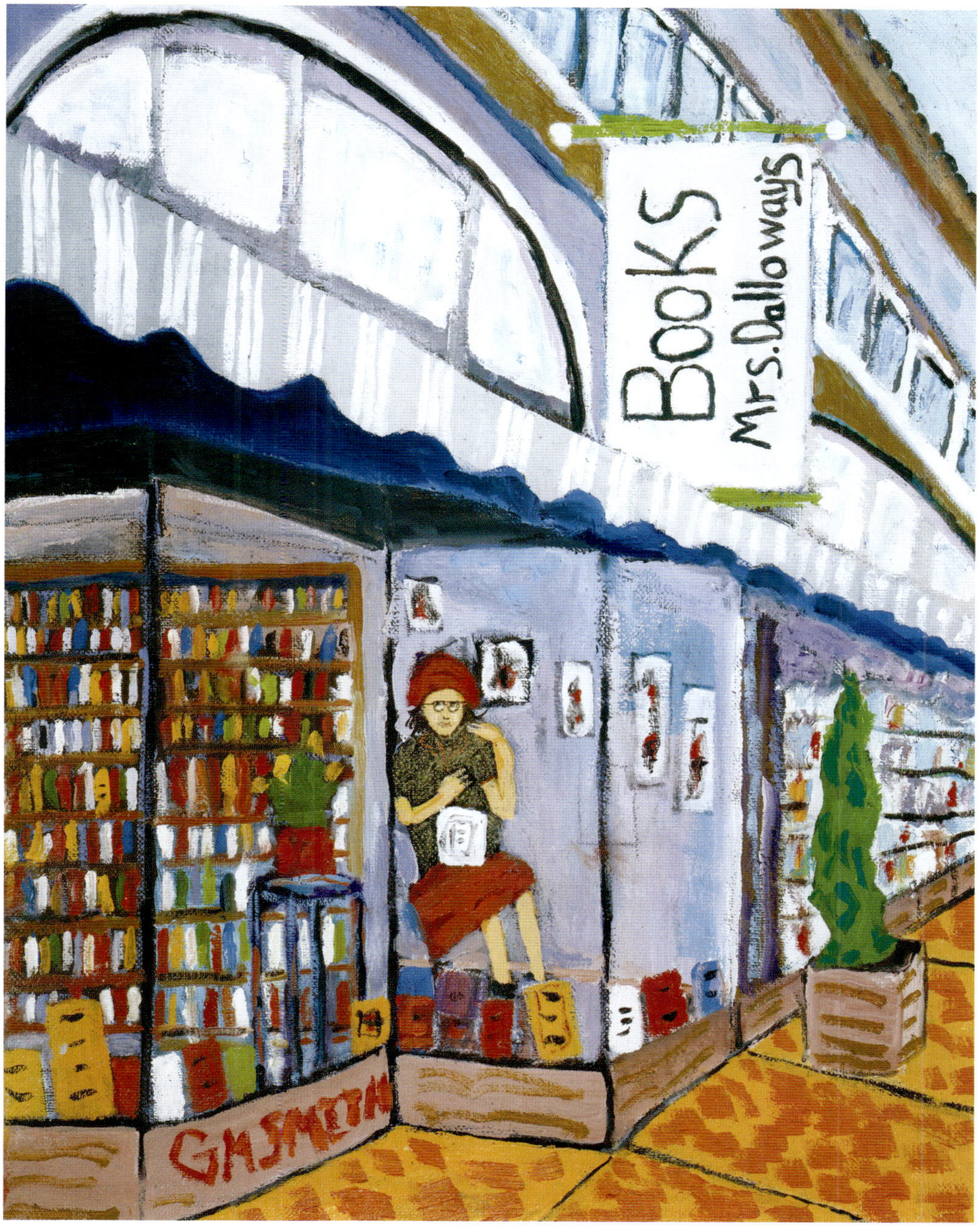

Gibbs M. Smith, Mrs. Dalloway's, 2008. *Oil on linen, 16" × 20".*

Page and Palette

FAIRHOPE, ALABAMA

Located at 32 South Section Street, Page and Palette was founded in 1968 by Betty Joe Wolff and is a well-known enclave for artists and writers. The store sells books as well as art supplies, and it has a charming coffee shop called Latte Da, which sells Southern favorite Blue Bell ice cream along with lattes and cappuccinos.

Today, the store is owned by Betty Joe's granddaughter Karin Wilson and Karin's husband, Kiefer. In addition to adding the coffee shop and a wonderful children's section to the store, Karin and Kiefer have established the Page and Palette Foundation, which does great things for their community. Page and Palette marked its 40th anniversary in 2008.

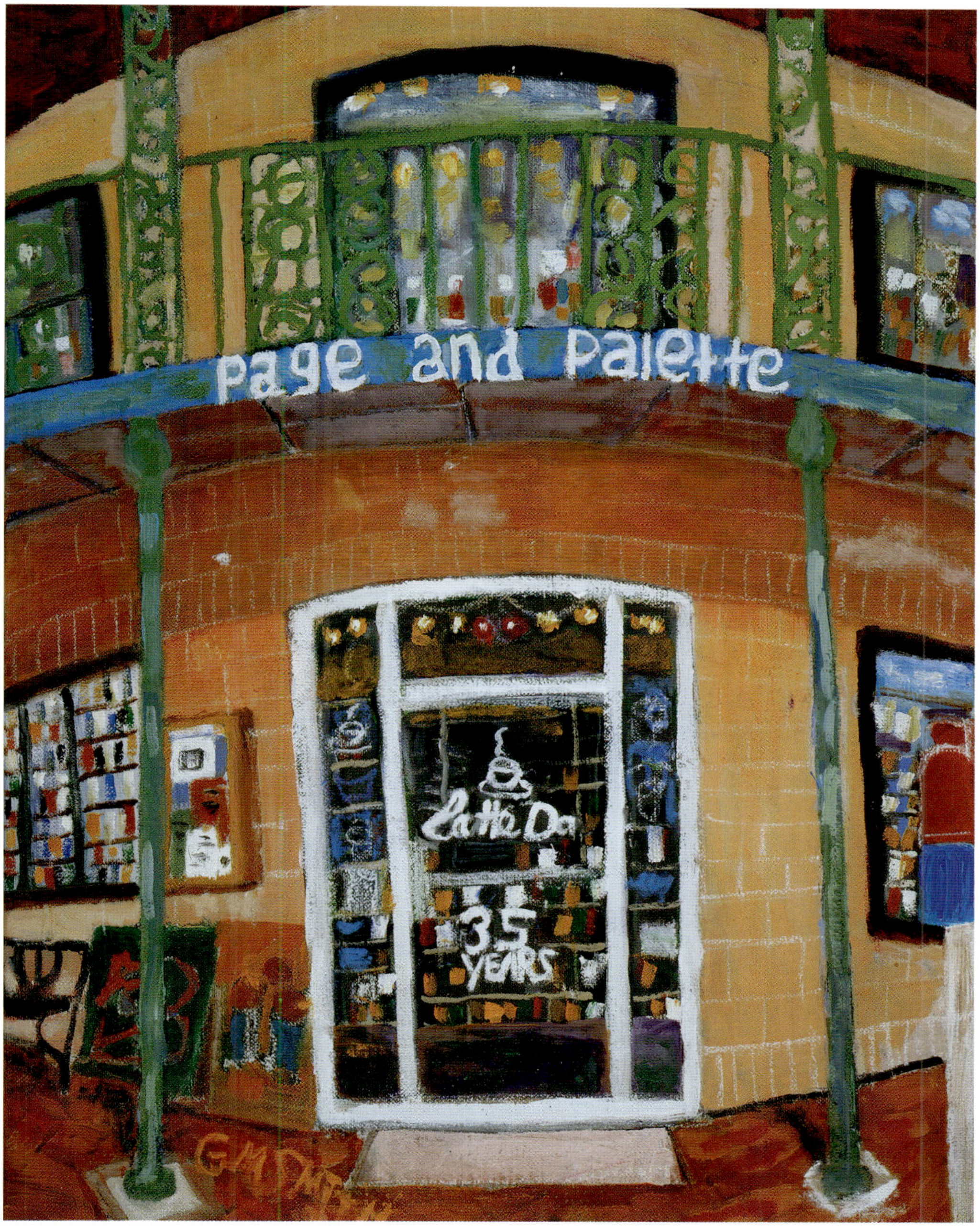

Gibbs M. Smith, Alabama Bookstore, 2007. *Oil on linen, 16" × 20".*

The King's English

SALT LAKE CITY, UTAH

Betsy Burton opened The King's English Bookstore in 1977 with then partner Ann Berman. When Berman left in 1985, Burton ran the store alone (with the help of many excellent booksellers) until 1987, when Barbara Hoagland became a partner. The King's English is well known and respected in the local community as well as the community of independent bookstores nationwide.

I have known Betsy for many years and have heard her speak about books to different audiences. She is a hands-on bookseller who does her homework. She reads at home and shares her knowledge and passion with customers about the books she sells. Customers rely on her opinion and are never disappointed. She is a wonderful bookseller and a valuable member of the bookselling community of our nation, and she understands the significant role independent bookstores have in their individual neighborhoods.

Betsy Burton, owner of The King's English Bookstore:

I truly believe that without independent businesses, a community withers and dies. Fortunately the indie movement is gaining ground all across the country, and independent bookstores are at the heart of that movement.

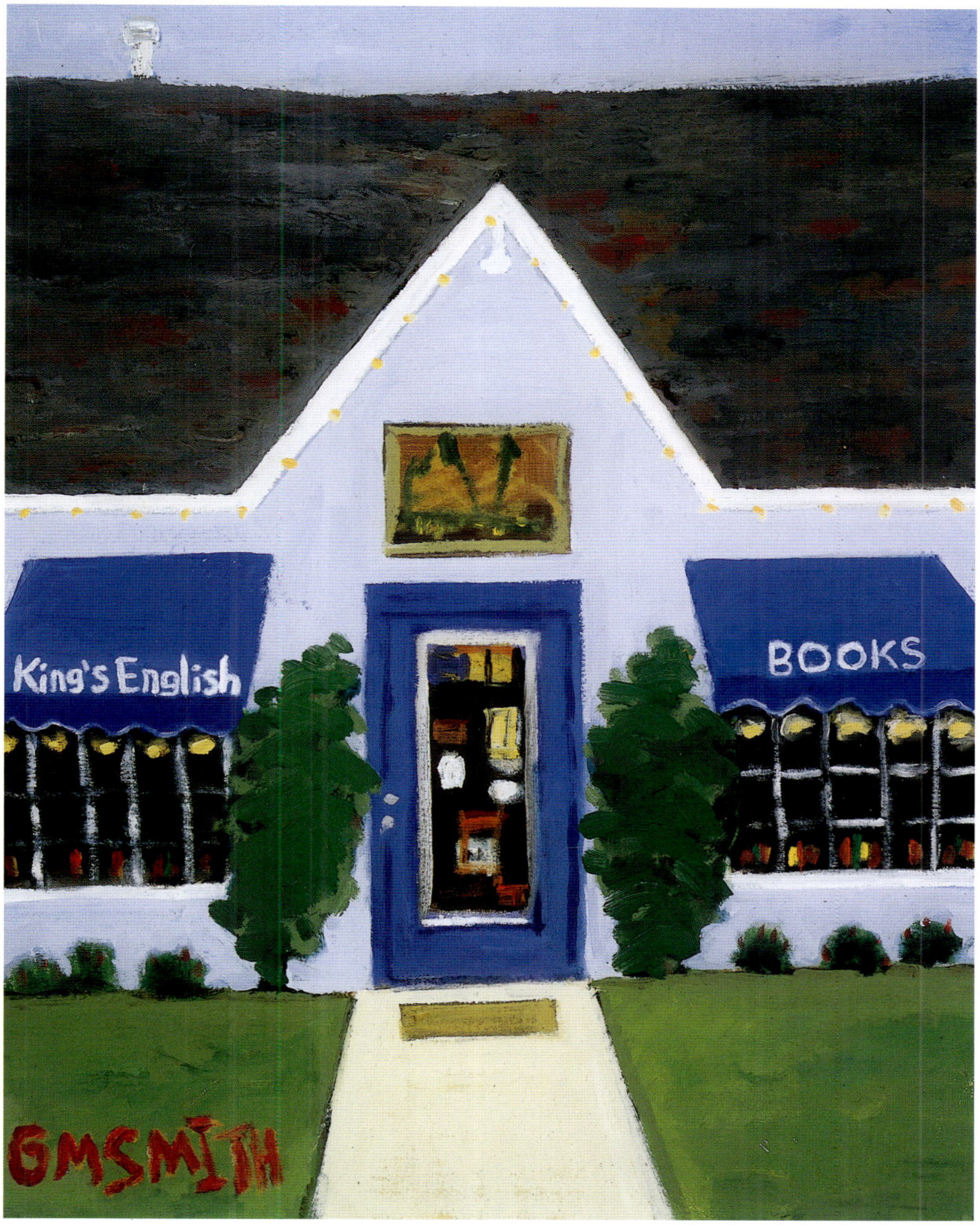

Gibbs M. Smith, Betsy's Bookstore, *2004. Oil on linen, 16" × 20".*

Politics and Prose Bookstore

WASHINGTON, D.C.

When I am in Washington, D.C., I always visit Politics and Prose, which was founded by Carla Cohen and Barbara Meade in 1984. This store has become one of the most honored independent bookstores in the country and has grown to twelve thousand square feet, with fifty employees. Politics and Prose has an impressive schedule of events, with authors and lectures occurring at least once a day. The store also has an impressive number of book groups that are led by the store's staff.

The name Politics and Prose fits with the clientele's interests, which include government and public policy, American history and biography, fiction, poetry, children's books, and much more.

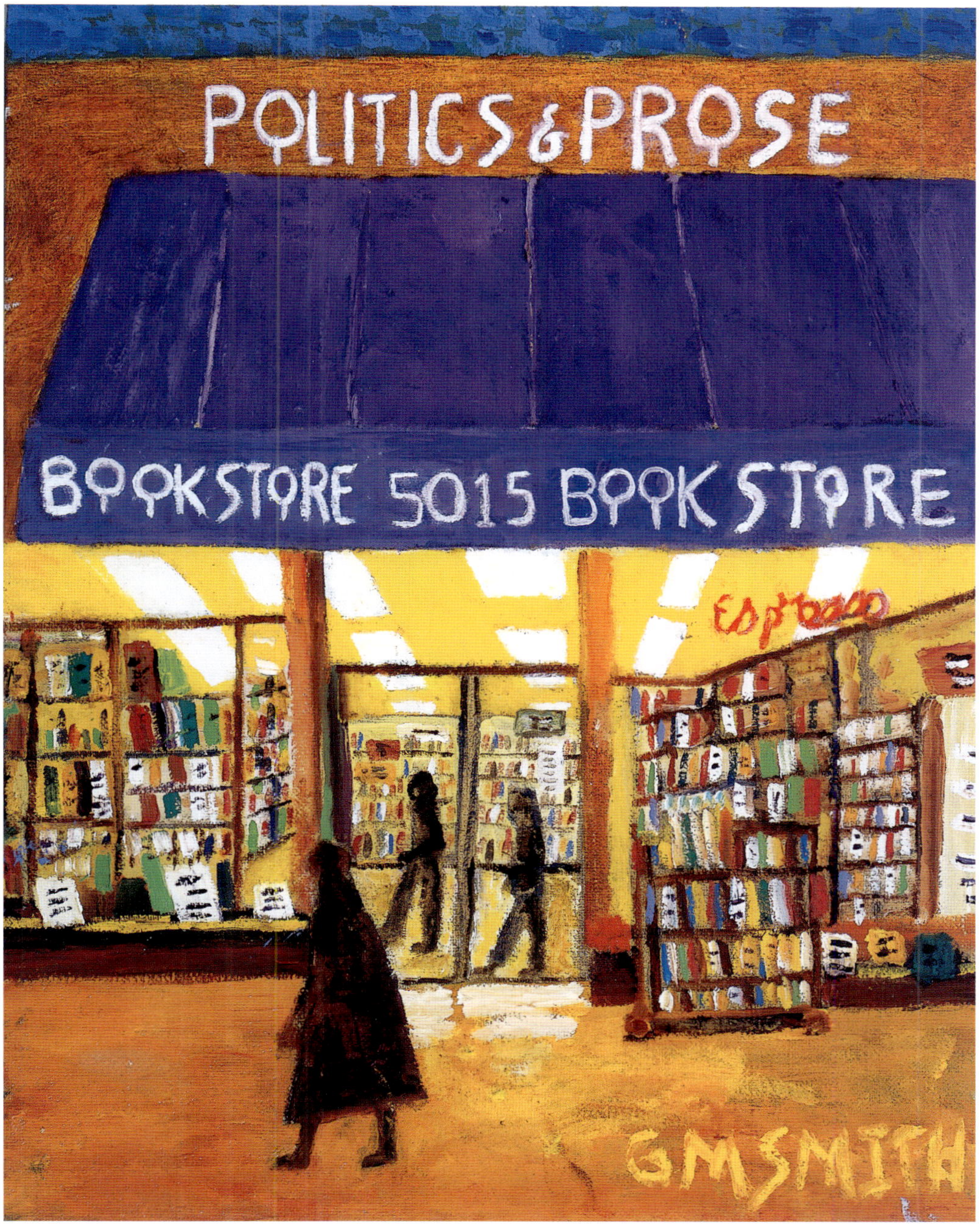

Gibbs M. Smith, Politics & Prose, *2006. Oil on linen, 16" × 20".*

Powell's Books

PORTLAND, OREGON

Founder and owner Michael Powell and his staff have created a great bookstore with Powell's. Michael began his career in bookselling in Chicago, where he opened a store selling used and rare books in 1970. Michael's father, Walter, was inspired to do the same and opened his own store in Portland in 1971. Michael ended up joining him after leaving Chicago. Walter had the crazy notion of selling used books—both paperbacks and hardbacks—along with new books. The idea worked, and Powell's has been a beloved Portland institution ever since.

A visit to Portland isn't complete without a visit to Powell's. The mammoth store, which takes up an entire city block with its thousands of books, is always buzzing with locals and tourists, who can end up browsing for hours. This painting of Powell's is at night, when the place is filled with intense and stimulating activity and romance.

Michael Powell, owner of Powell's Books:

We feel it's very important that the community have a thriving bookstore. We want people to see our stores as a resource where they can come and shop and feel relaxed, a place where they can come and be at the heart of the city. The community has come to respect the stores and see us as a city icon, and we take that responsibility very seriously.

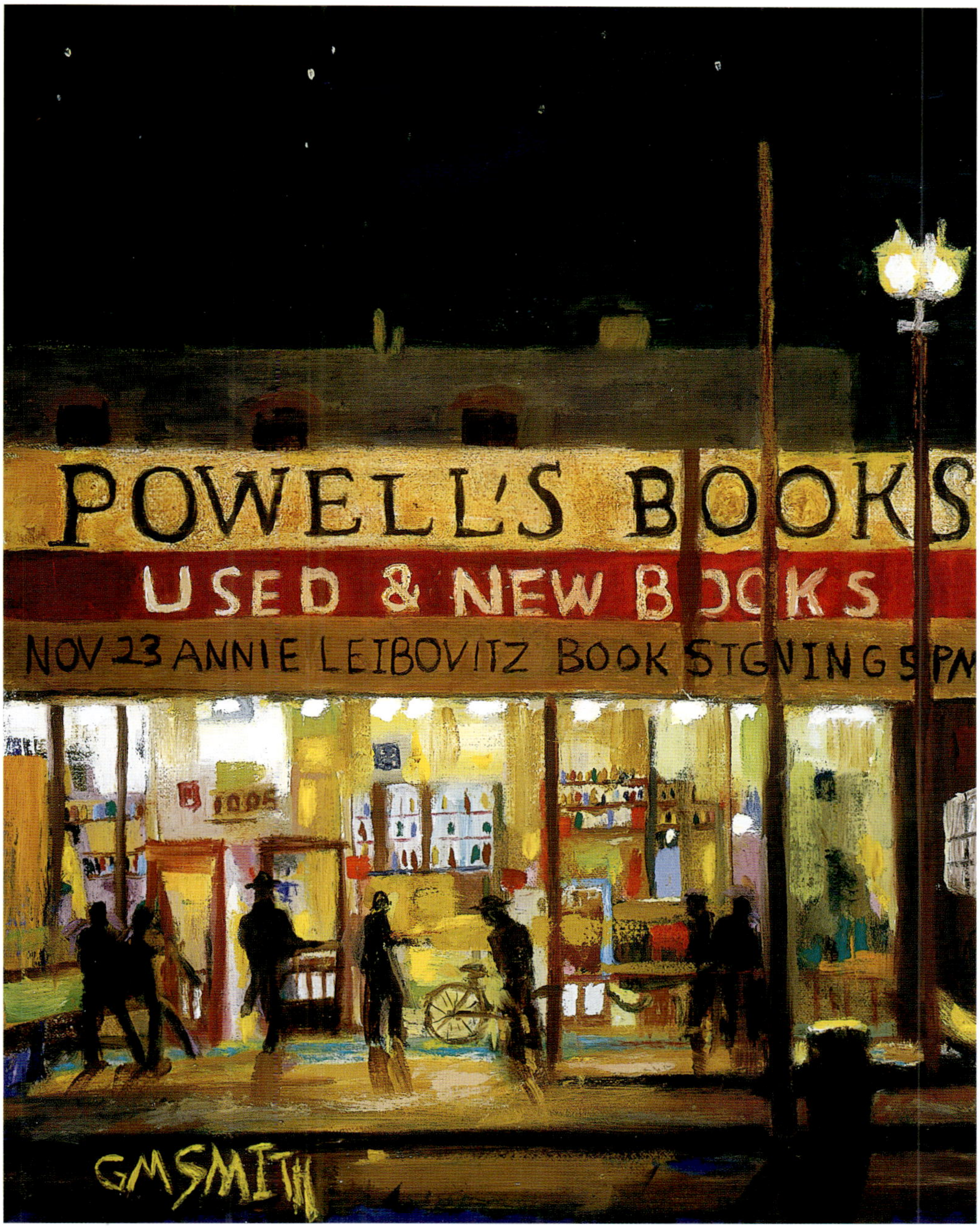

Gibbs M. Smith, Powell's, *2002. Oil on linen, 16" × 20".*

Changing Hands Bookstore

TUCSON, ARIZONA

by Gayle Shanks, co-owner of Changing Hands

Changing Hands began as a dream on the porch steps of an alternative school for kids where Tom Brodersen, Gayle Shanks, and Bob Sommer met each other as volunteers. One day we talked about what we'd really like to do with our lives and the idea that we hatched was a cozy, socially responsible bookstore and community gathering place. A few years later, Tom bought a small used bookstore for $500—all he had at the time—and asked his friends to help him. Changing Hands opened on April Fool's Day, 1974, with a big interest in books and community service.

I've always believed that a good bookstore is more than the books inside its walls. A good bookstore provides avid readers with a place not only to buy, but also to imbibe the essence of the magic of the written word. It exudes the passion of the booksellers, the desire by consumers for wonderful things to read, and the connection of those readers with authors and all things literary. A bookstore supports its reading community by bringing in authors so customers can 'hear' from them the sound of the very words they've written. It starts building readers by engaging children and their teachers in programs designed to inculcate the fun and value of reading at a very early age. It supports those readers as they grow by finding and sharing new books, new writers, new ideas with them through media, in-store displays, events, and story times. A bookstore builds a community around itself that supports and is supported by that community. It creates the literary landscape, it provides the space for the sharing of values, and is the underpinning of a free society where all ideas can be explored.

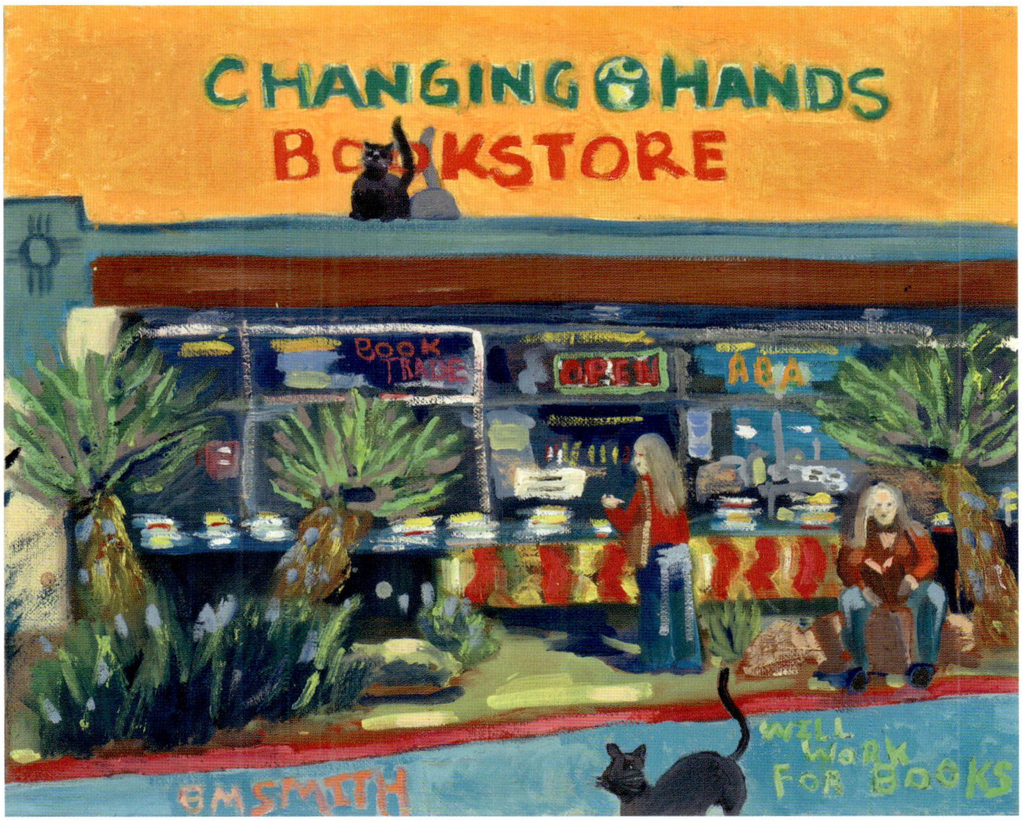

Gibbs M. Smith, Arizona Bookstore, *2009. Oil on linen, 16" × 20".*

Prairie Lights Books

IOWA CITY, IOWA

I first became aware of the tremendous literary vitality of Iowa City as a young graduate student in the 1960s. I was fortunate to have as a friend Wallace Stegner, who was then teaching at Stanford. He often shared with me stories of his life, and among his favorite experiences was the time he spent in Iowa City at the Iowa Writers' Workshop. He explained to me how important this institution is to the literary life of our country. The city is also home to the Iowa Playwrights' Workshop, the Iowa Summer Writing Festival, and the International Writing Program, and it has been designated by UNESCO as a City of Literature.

Prairie Lights Books built upon this rich literary tradition, opening in 1978 and devoting itself to fine literature, as well as nonfiction books, ever since. The owner, Jim Harris, has developed the store as a vital establishment in this literary corner of the world.

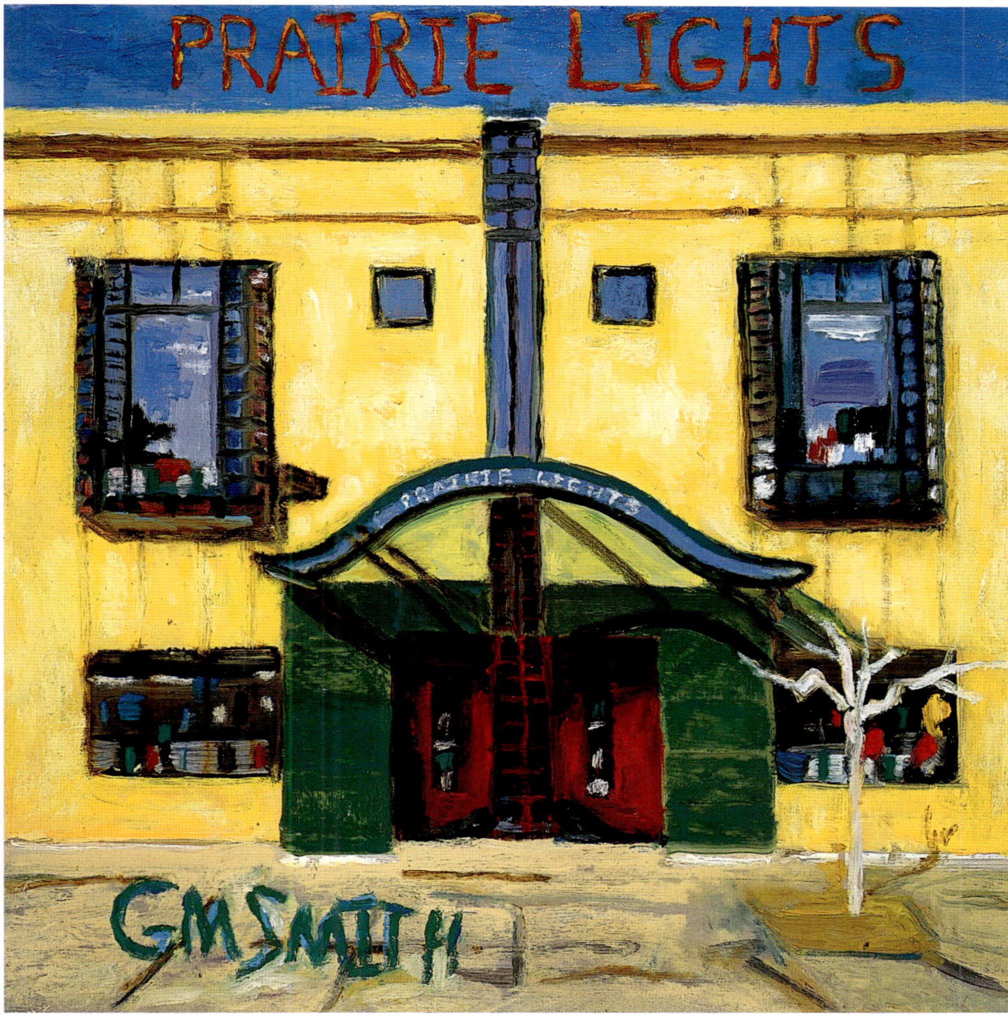

Gibbs M. Smith, Bookstore, Iowa City, *2004. Oil on linen, 16" × 20".*

Rizzoli Bookstore

NEW YORK CITY

This Manhattan book shop is the flagship store for Rizzoli, renowned publisher of art, architecture, interior design, fashion, photography, and other books on the visual arts, as well as travel, food and wine, humor, and children's books.

The origins of Rizzoli Bookstore's building at 31 West Fifty-Seventh Street between Fifth and Sixth avenues in New York City reach back to the late nineteenth century, when the structure was a private residence. It was one of many that lined both sides of Fifty-Seventh Street. Neighbors across the street included the families of James Roosevelt and Theodore Roosevelt, Sr., the father of President Theodore Roosevelt. Eventually the commercialization of nearby Fifth Avenue overflowed onto Fifty-Seventh Street. Because of Carnegie Hall's proximity, from 1890 onward piano manufacturers established their showrooms here. In the 1920s, 31 West Fifty-Seventh Street was altered to its present appearance for the Sohmer Piano Company. Since 1985, the building has served as the Rizzoli International Bookstore, the renowned purveyor of fine and unusual books on art, architecture, fashion, interior design, and related subjects.

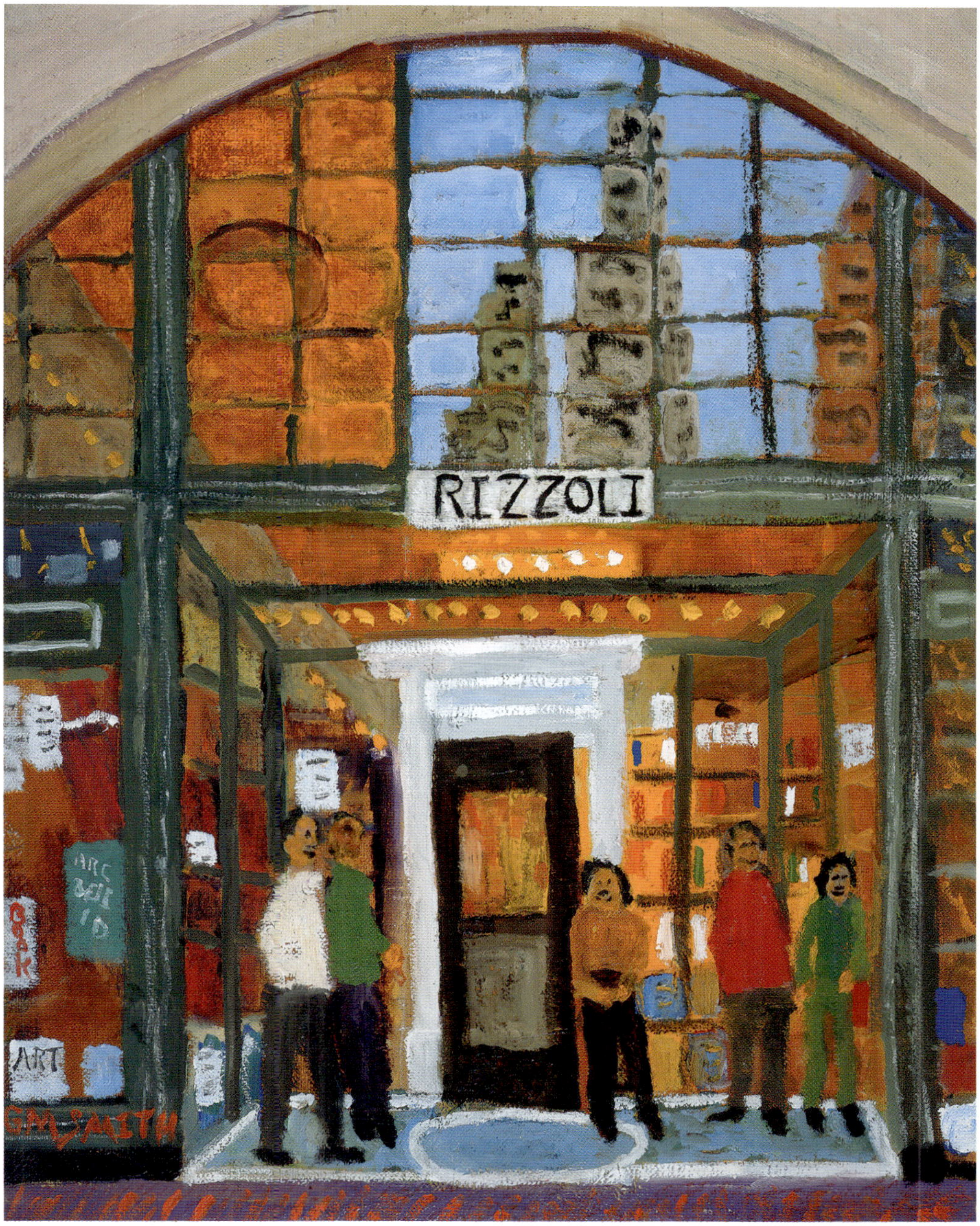

Gibbs M. Smith, New York, West Fifty-Seventh Street, *2007. Oil on linen, 16" × 20".*

R.J. Julia Independent Booksellers

MADISON, CONNECTICUT

R.J. Julia Booksellers, located on the shoreline of Madison, Connecticut, was founded by Roxanne Coady in 1989. The building originally housed Nick's Bar and Grill but was abandoned; it was covered in soot and grease when Roxanne purchased it. The store now consists of two buildings, including the R.J. Café and enough room to hold the more than two hundred author events presented each year.

The store is not named for one individual but is a combination: "R" for Roxanne, "J" for husband Kevin's middle name, and "Julia" for Roxanne's grandmother and source of inspiration.

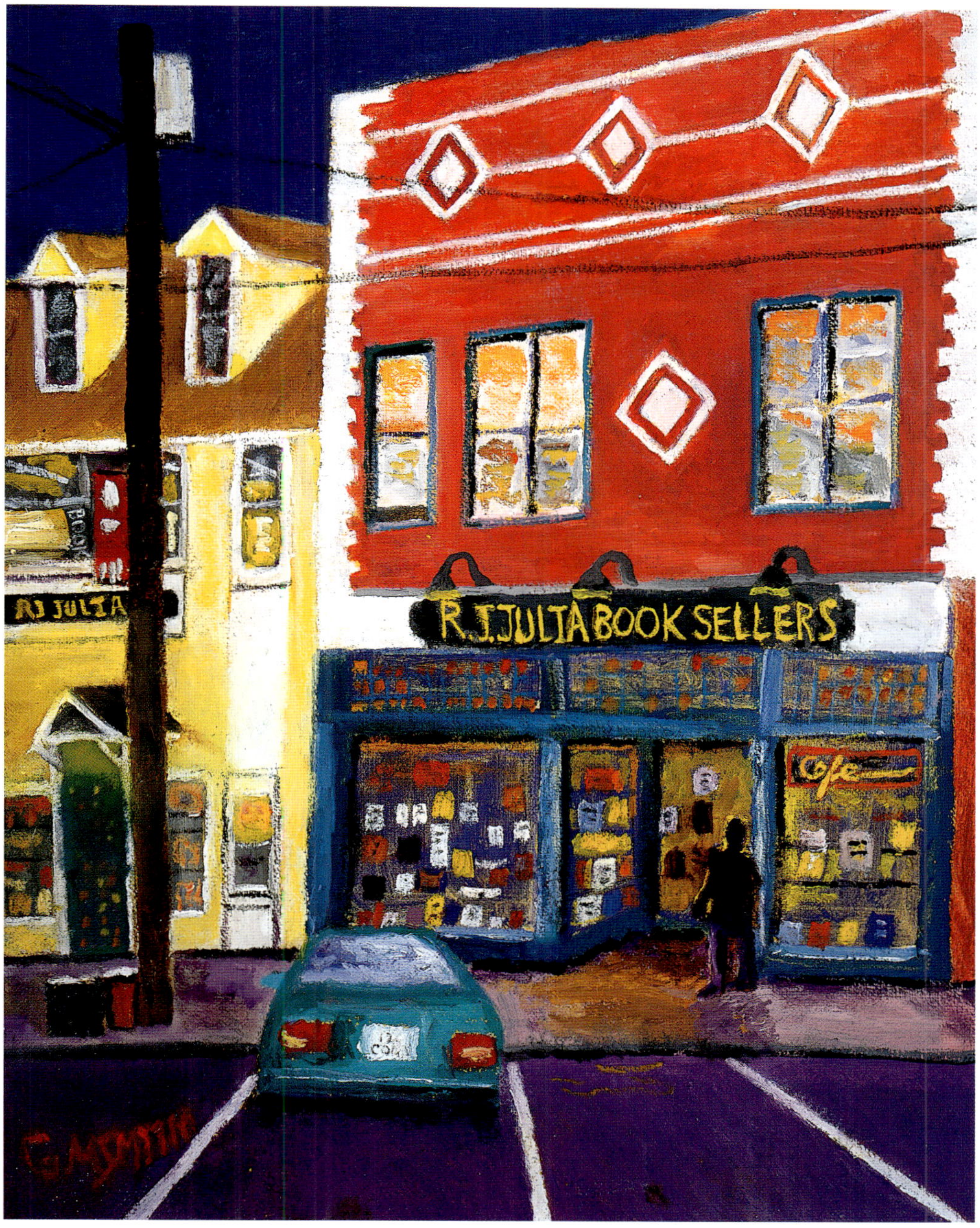

Gibbs M. Smith, R.J. Julia, *2006. Oil on linen, 16" × 20".*

Sam Weller's Zion Bookstore

SALT LAKE CITY, UTAH

I have known Weller's bookstore since 1948 when, as a child, my family moved from Oakland, California, to Utah. My mother and father took me to Weller's and helped me select books of my own. As I grew up, I returned and explored new titles and the store's enormous collection of used books. It was here that I first learned of publishing seasons, the bestseller list, readings by authors, and book signings. It was here I purchased many of the books that opened my mind—my first copies of Hemingway, Kerouac, Ferlinghetti, and many more. It was here that I met Wallace Stegner, Edward Abbey, Saul Bellow, and many others whom I came to love.

I recall my mother visited the store often, and Sam always called her by name and always found a new book especially for her. She was delighted, and I learned what personal bookselling was all about. Sam Weller's bookstore has been in business for sixty-seven years; it was founded by Gustav Weller, successfully nurtured by Sam and Lila Weller, and is now managed by Tony Weller. It is one of America's great bookselling institutions. Years ago, when I visited the old Scribners' store in New York City on Fifth Avenue, Igor Kropotkin, who managed the store, told me of the high regard he had for Sam Weller and what an important institution the Weller store was in the national bookselling world. I was very proud that my hometown had such a nationally significant business.

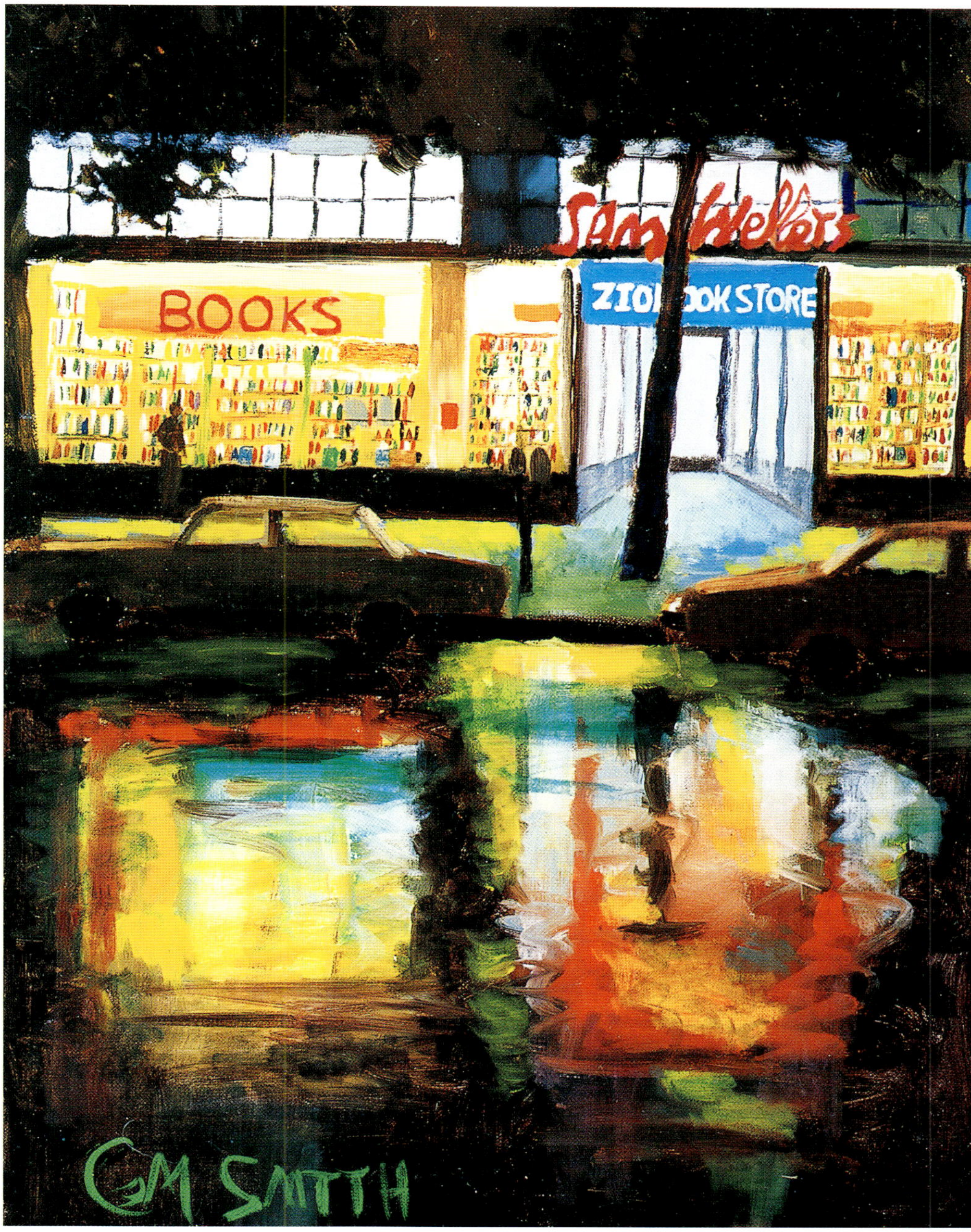

Gibbs M. Smith, Sam Weller's Bookstore in the Rain, *1996. Oil on linen, 16" × 20".*

Shakespeare & Co.

PARIS, FRANCE

Located across from Notre Dame Cathedral in Paris's Left Bank, Shakespeare & Co. is a cultural and social center for Parisians and visitors to the City of Lights. Shakespeare & Co. was founded in 1951 by George Whitman, then a student at the Sorbonne who had amassed a collection of English books during his studies. George took a cue from his friend Lawrence Ferlinghetti (poet, artist, and founder of City Lights Bookstore in San Francisco, California) and decided to open a bookstore. Since then, the store has welcomed writers, artists—and, indeed, anyone who walks through its doors—with open arms. Famous writers such as Henry Miller, James Baldwin, Langston Hughes, Anaïs Nin, and Allen Ginsberg browsed there, gave readings there, and even spent the night there—George keeps a room for traveling writers who need a place to stay.

The store is stocked floor-to-ceiling with books new and old. George encourages customers to stay and read all day if they like, and even borrow books if they can't afford to buy. Readings are held every Monday night, and aspiring writers can attend workshops in the store's upstairs library for a modest fee. Like the famous literary and artistic salons of the past, Shakespeare & Co. is an institution that nurtures writers, poets, and artists and cultivates contemplation and creativity.

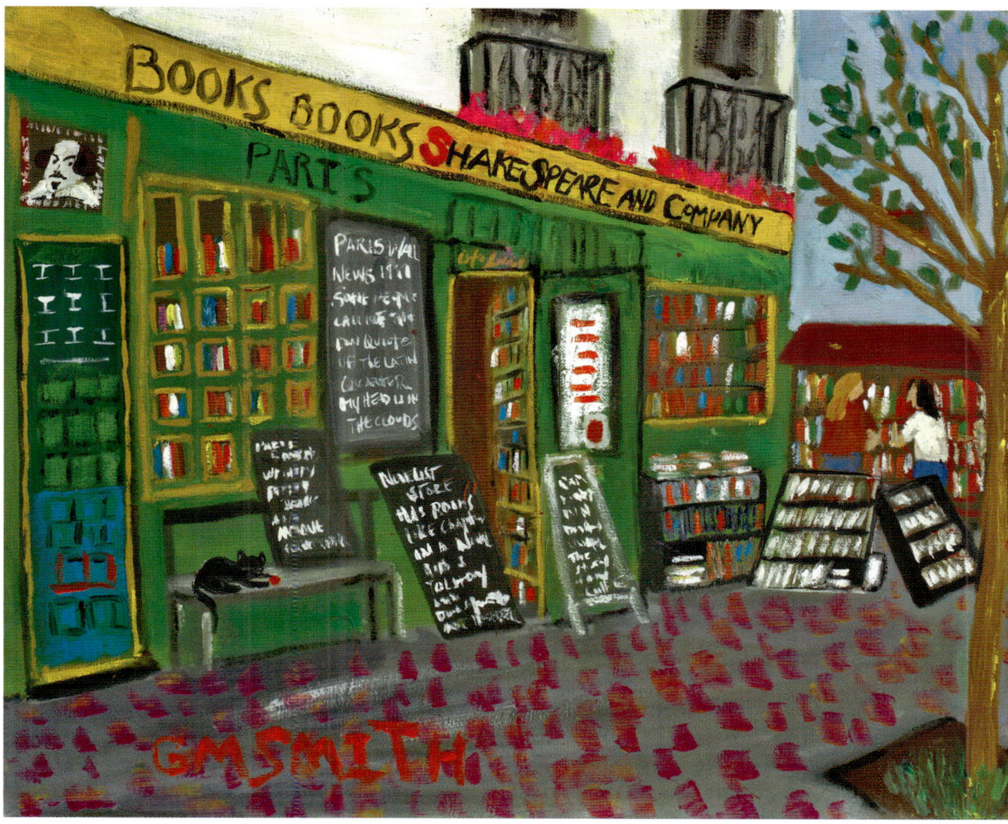

Gibbs M. Smith, Paris in the Spring, *2009. Oil on linen, 16" × 20".*

Tattered Cover Book Store

DENVER, COLORADO

The Tattered Cover was founded in 1971 by Joyce Meskis. There are three Tattered Cover locations: one at Colfax Avenue, one at Highlands Ranch, and the store that I have painted in LoDo. I frequent this store often, as I like traveling by train and this store is located a block from the train station. It is one of my favorite places to visit and stock up on books, after which I hop back on the train and enjoy reading as I travel either east or west.

Buying books was a way anyone could acquire a work of art for very little.

—Sol LeWitt

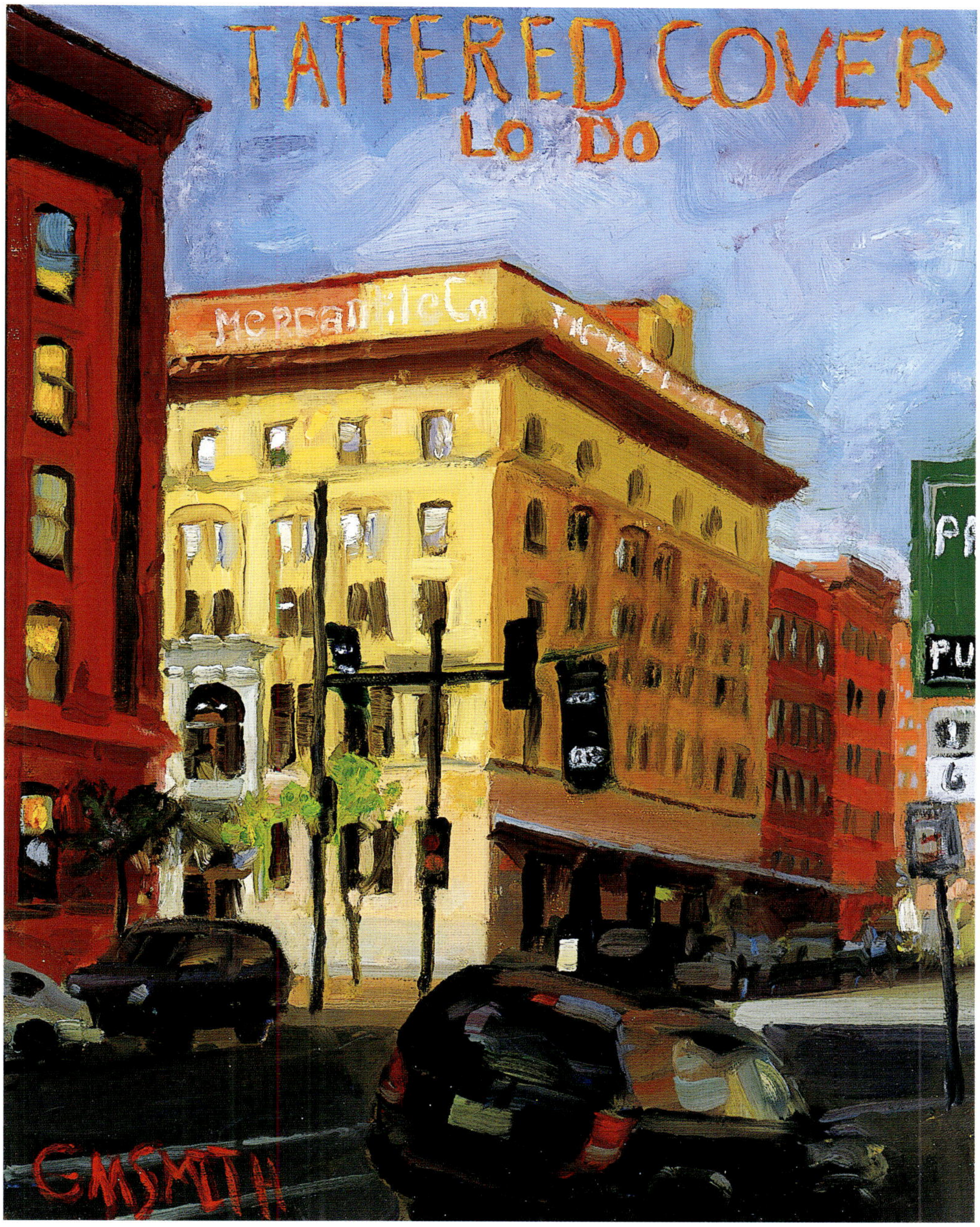

Gibbs M. Smith, The Tattered Cover Book Store, *2002. Oil on linen, 16" × 20".*

Skylight Books

LOS ANGELES, CALIFORNIA

by Kerry Slattery, general manager and co-owner of Skylight Books

Skylight Books is in the heart of the lively, artsy Los Feliz neighborhood of Los Angeles, between Hollywood and downtown, next door on one side to a busy independent movie theatre and on the other side to a theatre and acting school, with small restaurants and quirky shops all along the street. It is located in a 1930s building with a fascinating old high-beamed ceiling, and there's a twenty-foot-high ficus tree in the middle of the store that seems to thrive because it's right under industrial skylights.

Before we opened in 1996, there had been another bookstore in the same site for over twenty years, Chatterton's, which was known for its smart poetry and independent press selections. The store closed in 1994 when the owner died of AIDS in his forties. (The poet Billy Collins once told me that when he was in college at Riverside, he and his pals used to come to L.A. because Chatterton's was the only place that carried his handmade chapbooks on consignment.)

Milton Katselas, the acting teacher from the acting school next door, felt passionately that the neighborhood still really needed a bookstore and, against all advice from friends that it was a terrible time to open an independent bookstore, we found ten other people to each put up a small portion of the investment needed, including a retired English teacher, owners of a local family restaurant, a voice teacher, a playwright, several actors, and a geologist, most of whom still do not know one another. I have run the bookstore from the beginning, and our store buyer and manager have both been here for that time as well.

Even though Skylight has developed its own unique personality over the years, our customers who remember the old Chatterton's feel that we have kept the spirit alive of the bookstore where Ginsberg once came to do readings.

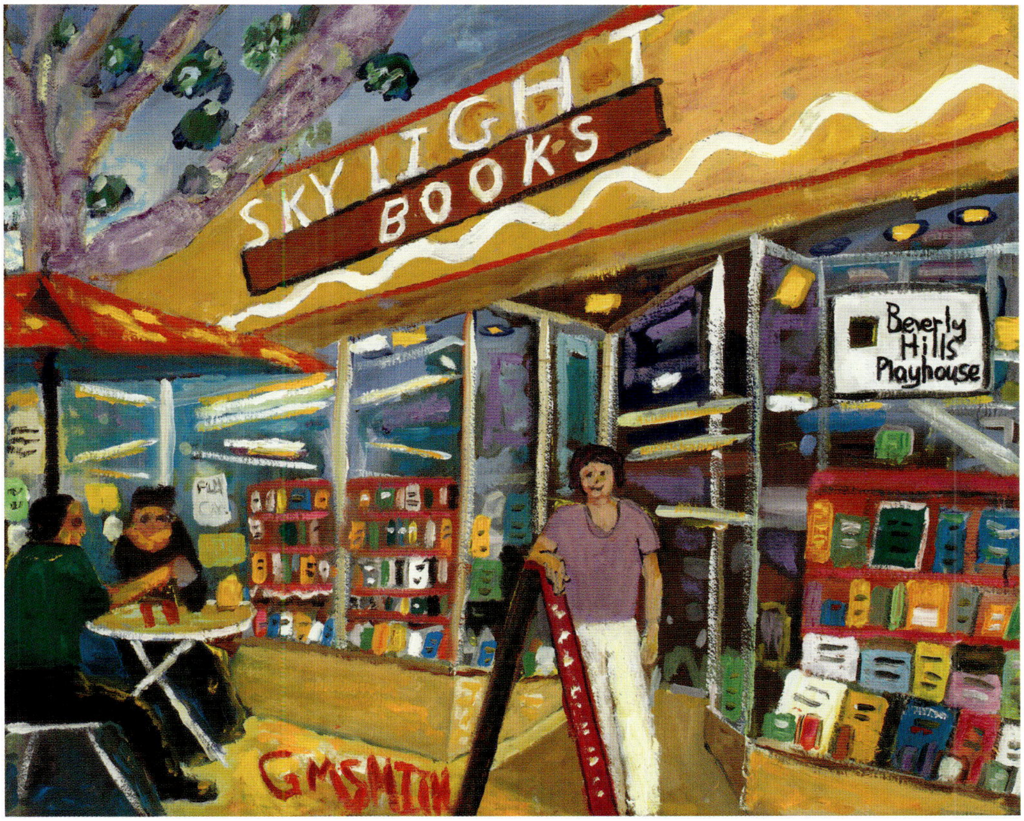

Gibbs M. Smith, Los Feliz, Los Angeles, *2009. Oil on linen, 16" × 20".*

Books & Books

CORAL GABLES, FLORIDA

Books & Books was founded by Mitchell Kaplan. The store is a local landmark as well as a gathering place for readers and aspiring writers alike. Housed in an exquisite 1927 building listed in the Coral Gables Register of Historic Places, the Mediterranean-style building has original tile floors, fireplace, beamed ceilings, floor-to-ceiling bookshelves, and an open-air courtyard with a full-service café. Books & Books hosts over fifty events a month, consisting of author appearances, readings, demonstrations, lectures, children's activities, and a variety of other community-based programs.

Mitchell Kaplan , owner of Books & Books:

For me, the art of bookselling begins and ends with the notion of serving your community. Everything I do as a bookstore owner is an attempt to create that great, good place, where service, selection, and ambiance come together to celebrate the richness and diversity of literary culture, all the while providing a unique space where there is comfort in knowing that the free flow of ideas is honored and respected. Redefining the way our customer measures value is the tool by which Books & Books has been able to reassert this idea of the primacy of the third place. Value should not be measured only in terms of price; value, instead, has to be calculated by how well we serve our community, and how well we express this to our customer. The distinctive selection of books we carry, the readings, lectures and demonstrations we mount, the commitment to fostering a love of books and reading in children and teens, our next generation of readers, the sharing of our public space with community groups, from Amnesty International to a Tibetan Buddhist study collective, this is the value that we provide our community. And, it's most fortunate for us, in this very, very difficult climate for independent bookstores, that our community has responded, reaffirming their desire for the kind of a place that is Books & Books.

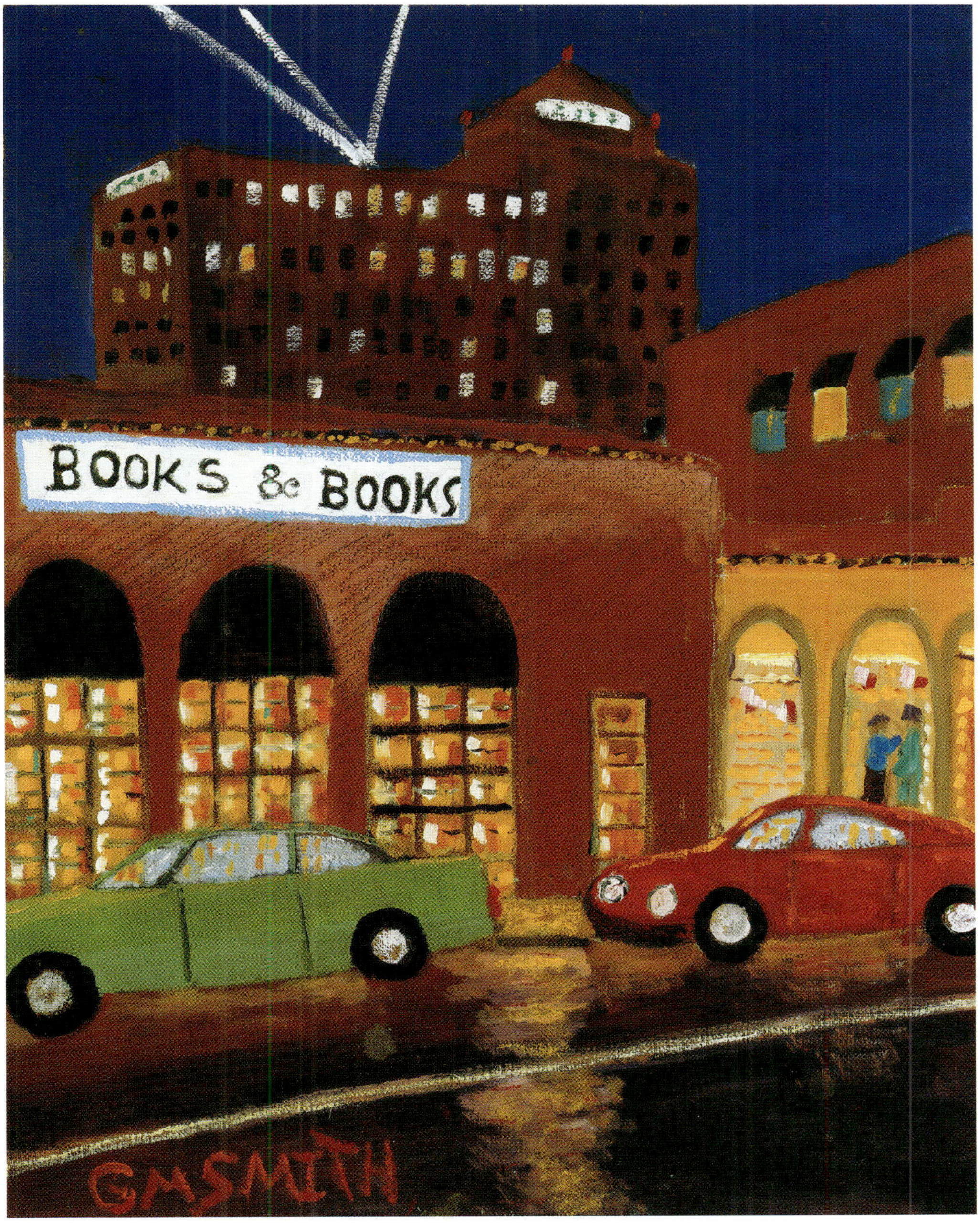

Gibbs M. Smith, Books & Books—Coral Gables, Florida, *2007. Oil on linen, 18" × 24".*

Builders Booksource

BERKELEY, CALIFORNIA

by George and Sally Kiskaddon, partners, Builders Booksource

We started Builders Booksource with high hopes, seeing part of our mission as bringing together two disparate groups we targeted as a significant part of our market—architects and builders. Builders Booksource provides a venue where these professionals mix, where questions are raised and problems solved. Over the years, our reputation as a resource has grown. In today's information-jammed society, where books are often considered just another commodity, we continue to see our role as problem solvers, not only for the professionals we cater to, but also for the lay people that frequent our street. We and our customers have found that books are so much more than a commodity—they inspire and teach, provide confidence and direction, and in the end become that comfortable presence on our bookshelf, ready to be drawn on again and again. As booksellers, we take tremendous pride and enjoyment from helping our customers answer that question, solve that problem. As difficult as the business of bookselling is these days, we continue to be inspired by and enjoy the process.

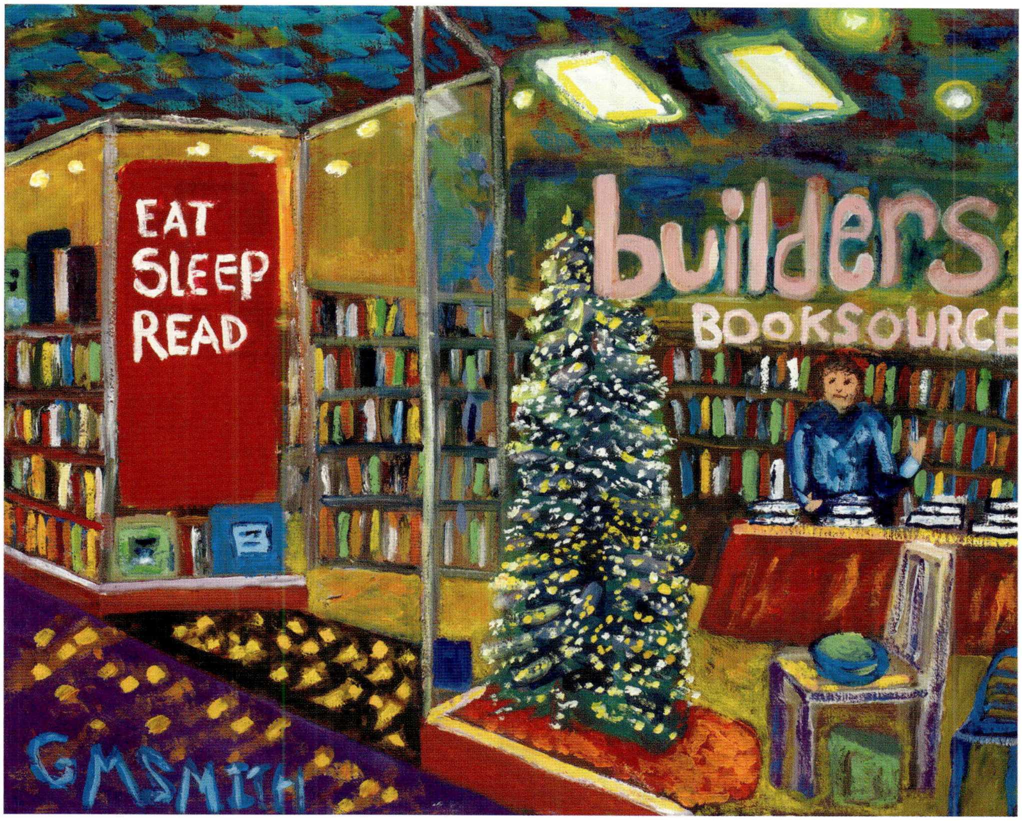

Gibbs M. Smith, Christmas on Fourth Street, Berkeley, *2009. Oil on linen, 16" × 20".*

St. Mark's Bookshop

NEW YORK CITY

This modern shop located in the East Village near New York University was opened in 1977 by Terry McCoy and Bob Contant. Terry and Bob keep their store alive and relevant by responding to their clientele with carefully selected, specialized titles that are difficult to find in other stores. The shelves are stocked with books on graphic design, music, art, film, poetry, and indie literature. They have an impressively large critical theory section, with titles that would not necessarily fare as well in other stores but that customers at St. Mark's want. The knowledgeable staff always has interesting recommendations. I enjoy browsing here because I always discover something new.

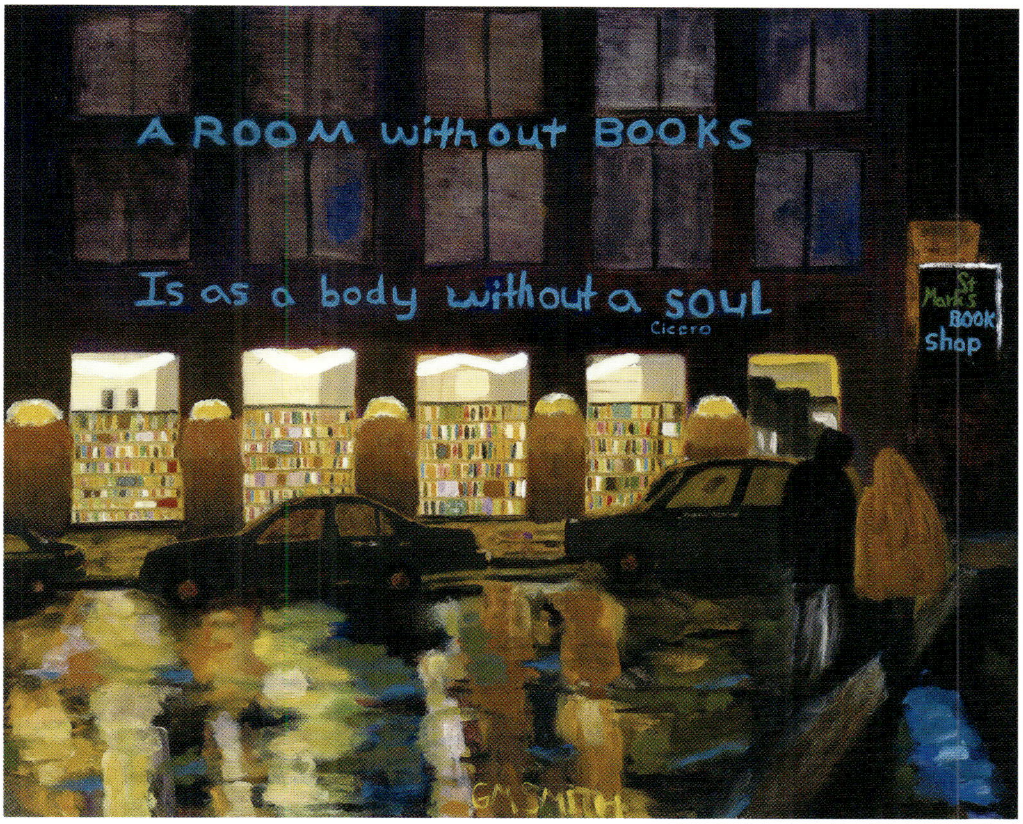

Gibbs M. Smith, St. Mark's Bookstore in the Rain, *1995. Oil on linen, 20" × 30".*

Tecolote Book Shop

SANTA BARBARA, CALIFORNIA

Opened in 1925 in the Montecito area of Santa Barbara, the beloved Tecolote Book Shop was in danger of closing in 2007 after eighty-two years in business. But Mary Sheldon, the manager at the time, knew how important the independent store was to the community and wanted to do everything she could to help save it. She found three willing partners, Len Freedman, Marc Winkelman, and longtime customer Herb Simon, to help her purchase the shop from then-owner Peggy Dent. Mary was able to save this local treasure, and the community proudly supports it by shopping there as their parents and grandparents did.

Mary and her two employees are exceptionally knowledgeable about books and are happy to make recommendations or locate elusive out-of-print titles.

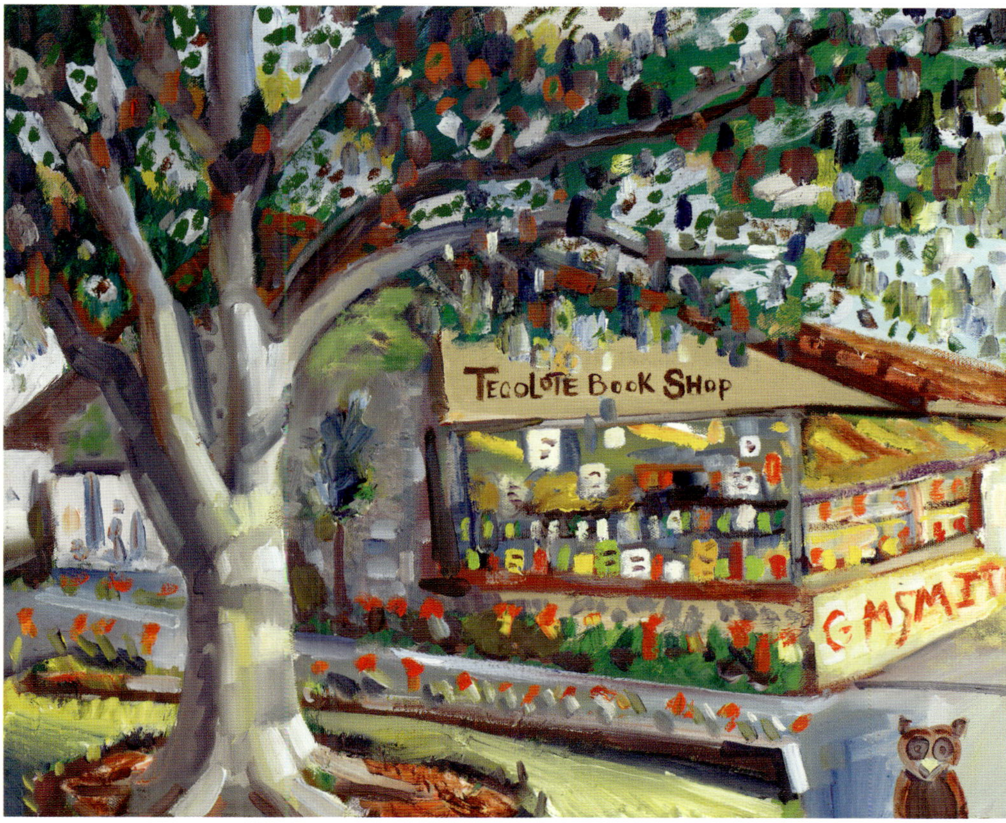

Gibbs M. Smith, Santa Barbara in the Spring, *2009. Oil on linen, 16" × 20".*

That Bookstore in Blytheville

BLYTHEVILLE, ARKANSAS

That Bookstore in Blytheville is owned by Mary Gay Shipley, a native of Blytheville, who opened the store in 1976. After customers had called it "that bookstore" for years, Mary Gay officially named it as such in 1994.

Over the years, the store has become a center for Arkansas Delta culture. It carries more than 25,000 titles. Mary Gay is a wonderful citizen in her community, helping with the Head Start program in the surrounding schools and hosting folk concerts in the back room of the store. Customers will note that the wooden chairs in the store have been signed by visiting authors. The store also houses an antique woodstove that is a popular place to nestle up to during the winter. Legend has it that That Bookstore in Blytheville is one of John Grisham's favorites.

My home is where my books are.

—Ellen Thompson

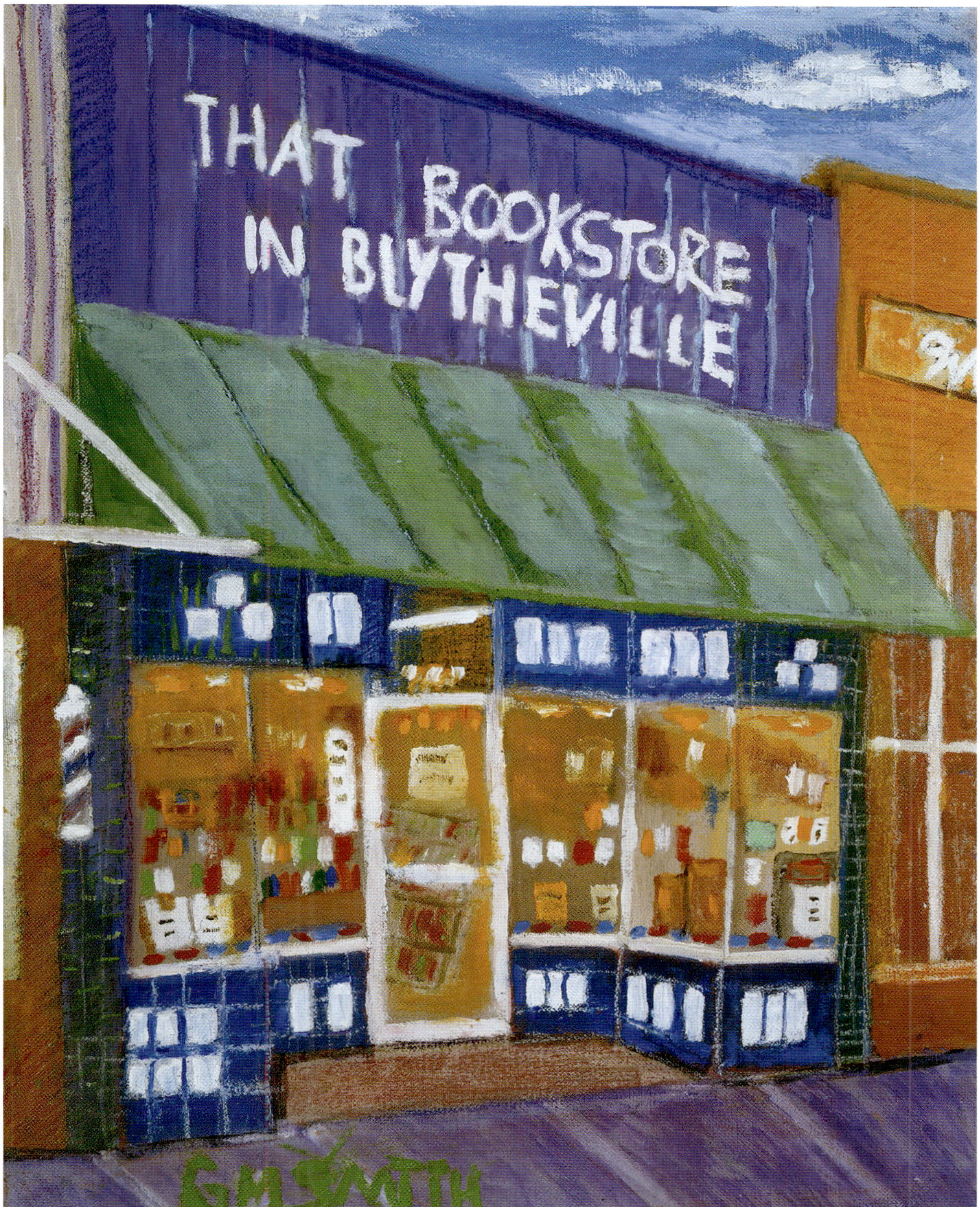

Gibbs M. Smith, That Bookstore in Blytheville—Blytheville, Arkansas, *2007.*
Oil on linen, 16" × 20".

Three Lives & Company

NEW YORK CITY

Located in New York's Greenwich Village, Three Lives & Company was founded in 1978 by a group of three friends, Jenny Feder, Helene Webb, and Jill Dunbar. In 2001, the owners sold the store to Toby Cox, who was then working at Random House. Toby jumped at the chance, feeling that Three Lives was exactly the kind of bookstore he would want to own. He carries the sorts of things that he and his staff like to read—fiction, poetry, biography, travel, art.

This bookstore is a rare place. Its shelves are intentionally left unlabeled so that you'll approach its friendly staff, hopefully ending up in a lively conversation about books. Its displays are arranged artistically, and you get the feeling that the staff has a real regard for books not only as vessels for information, but also as physical objects, as works of art. That is something that speaks to me, as we at Gibbs Smith feel that we handcraft each of the books we publish.

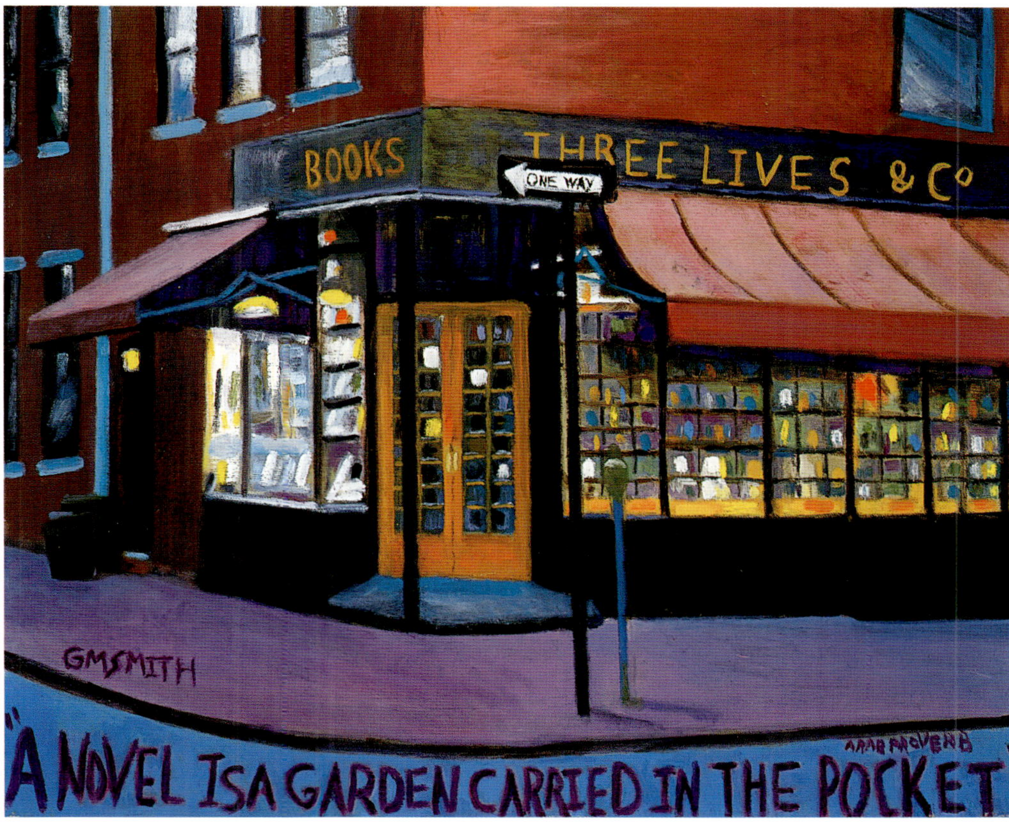

Gibbs M. Smith, Three Lives Bookstore, Greenwich Village, *1993. Oil on canvas, 16" × 20".*

Village Books

BELLINGHAM, WASHINGTON

Dee and Chuck Robinson founded Village Books on June 20, 1980, after traveling the West Coast from the Canadian border to just north of the Bay Area looking for a place to start a bookstore. They explored place after place before settling on the Fairhaven neighborhood of Bellingham, Washington.

Over the years the store has expanded several times, going from 1,500 square feet to about 10,000 in its current space. The new store space also opens into Paper Dreams, a card and gift store owned by Dee and Chuck, and includes two cafés—the Colophon Café and Book Fare. With the move, used books and remainders were also integrated into all sections of the store.

Chuck and Dee are very involved in their community and in the bookselling world. They have both served on boards of notable bookselling associations and participate actively in local organizations that aid community members. Village Books was named the 2008 Outstanding Philanthropic Small Business in the State of Washington.

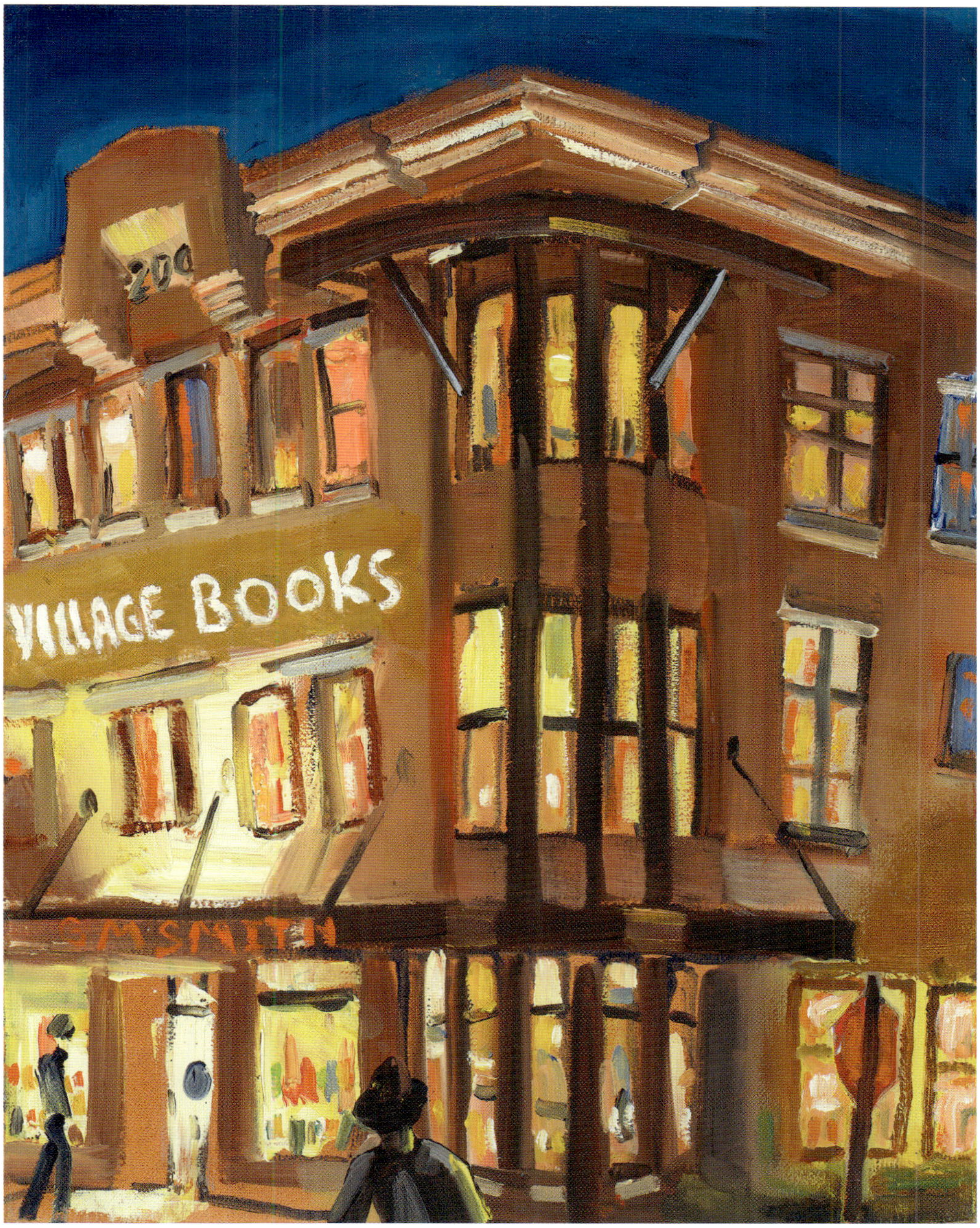

Gibbs M. Smith, On the Way to Alaska, *2009. Oil on linen, 16" × 20".*

Vroman's Bookstore

PASADENA, CALIFORNIA

Adam Clark Vroman, the well-known photographer who specialized in images of Native Americans and of the Southwest, founded Vroman's Bookstore in 1894. This makes Vroman's one of the oldest continuously operating independent bookstores in America.

When I was a child in Pasadena in the 1940s, my mother would often take me to Vroman's, where we explored their fine collection. Vroman's main store has always been in Pasadena, but it has had several satellite locations throughout its history. The store has had strong community ties and it currently has a program whereby customers who choose to can have a percent of the proceeds of their purchases go to worthy Pasadena charities.

Where is human nature so weak as in the bookstore?

—Henry Ward Beecher

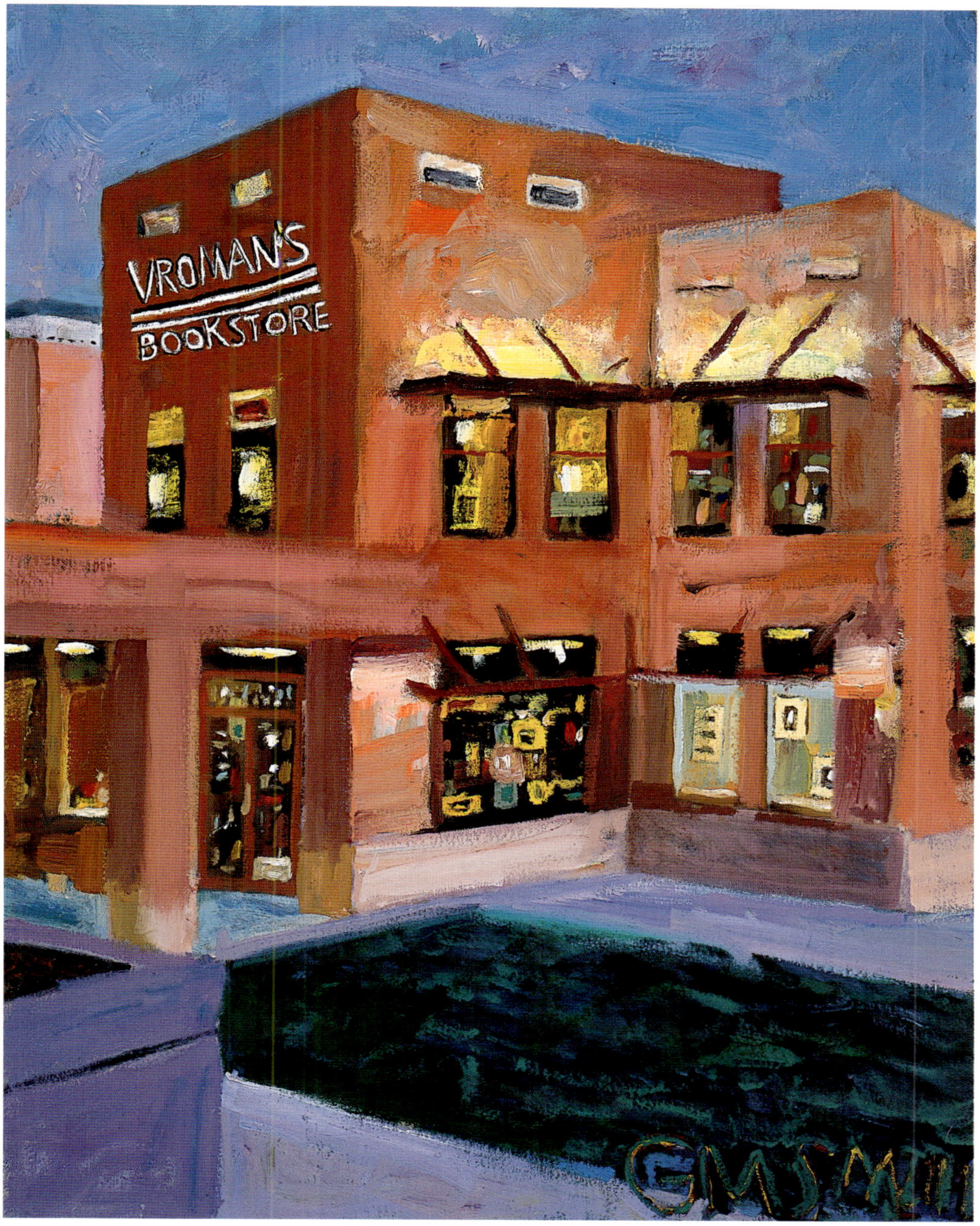

Gibbs M. Smith, Vroman's Bookstore, *2003. Oil on linen, 16" × 20".*

Warwick's

LA JOLLA, CALIFORNIA

In 1896, W. T. Warwick began a business in Minnesota, selling books as well as stationery and writing instruments. When he moved to California in the 1930s, he brought the business with him and opened a store in downtown La Jolla. Warwick's has been there ever since and has gone through four generations. It is currently run by W. T. Warwick's great-granddaughters, Nancy and Cathy Warwick, and the store has expanded to include a diverse array of attractive products in addition to books and writing tools, including home décor and jewelry.

Warwick's is a vital part of the community, hosting author signings and reading groups, and participating in other events to get the community excited about reading. Warwick's takes part in One Book, One San Diego, a program hosted by the San Diego Public Library and a local radio station that encourages all of San Diego to become one big book club by reading the same book at the same time. Books for Schools is a Warwick's program that invites schoolchildren, parents, and staff to attend author readings of children's books; a portion of the sales from that author event then go to the school.

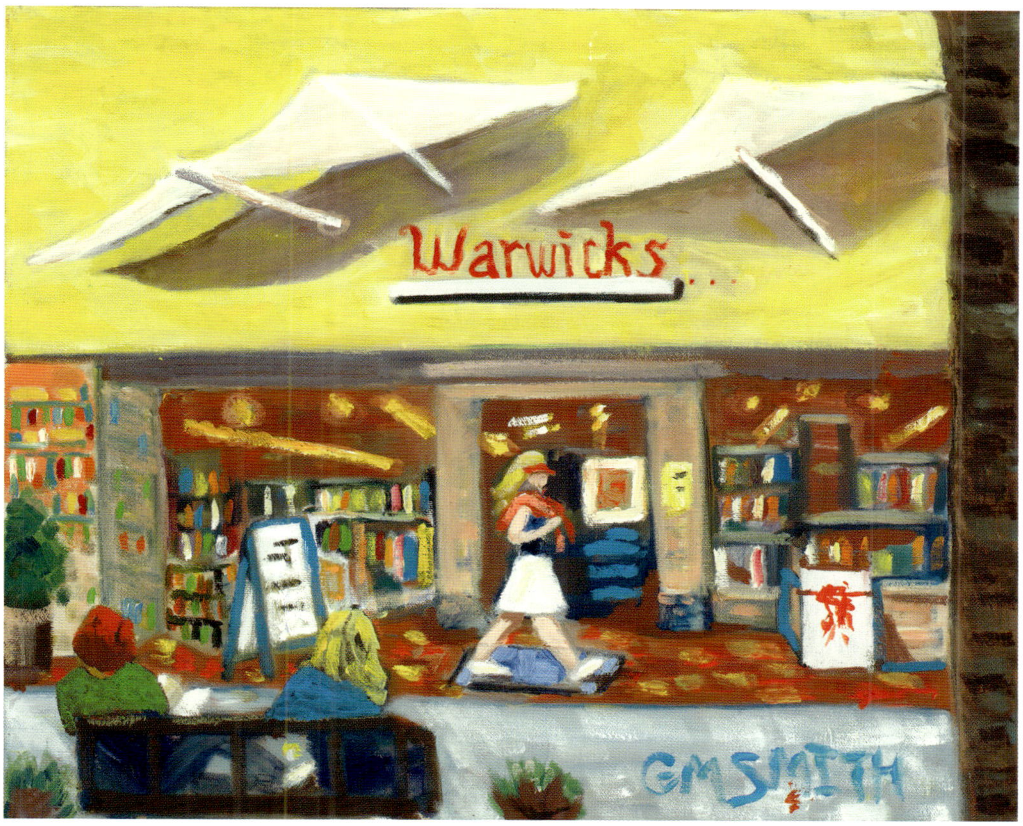

Gibbs M. Smith, Warwick's, *2009. Oil on linen, 16" × 20".*

Watermark Books & Café

WICHITA, KANSAS

Watermark Books in Wichita, Kansas, is owned by Sara Bagley and Bruce Jacobs and was founded in 1977. It is located in the College Hill neighborhood of Wichita, which has many historic homes and a marvelous shopping area where Watermark and its ancient elm tree have been located these many years.

Watermark is known for its friendly staff, its frequent author events, its book clubs, and its café, serving coffee, pastries, and salads, along with sandwiches such as the Moby Dick (tuna salad) and Dante's Inferno (roast beef, red peppers, and pepper jack cheese). Watermark Books & Café is a gathering place for the members of its community.

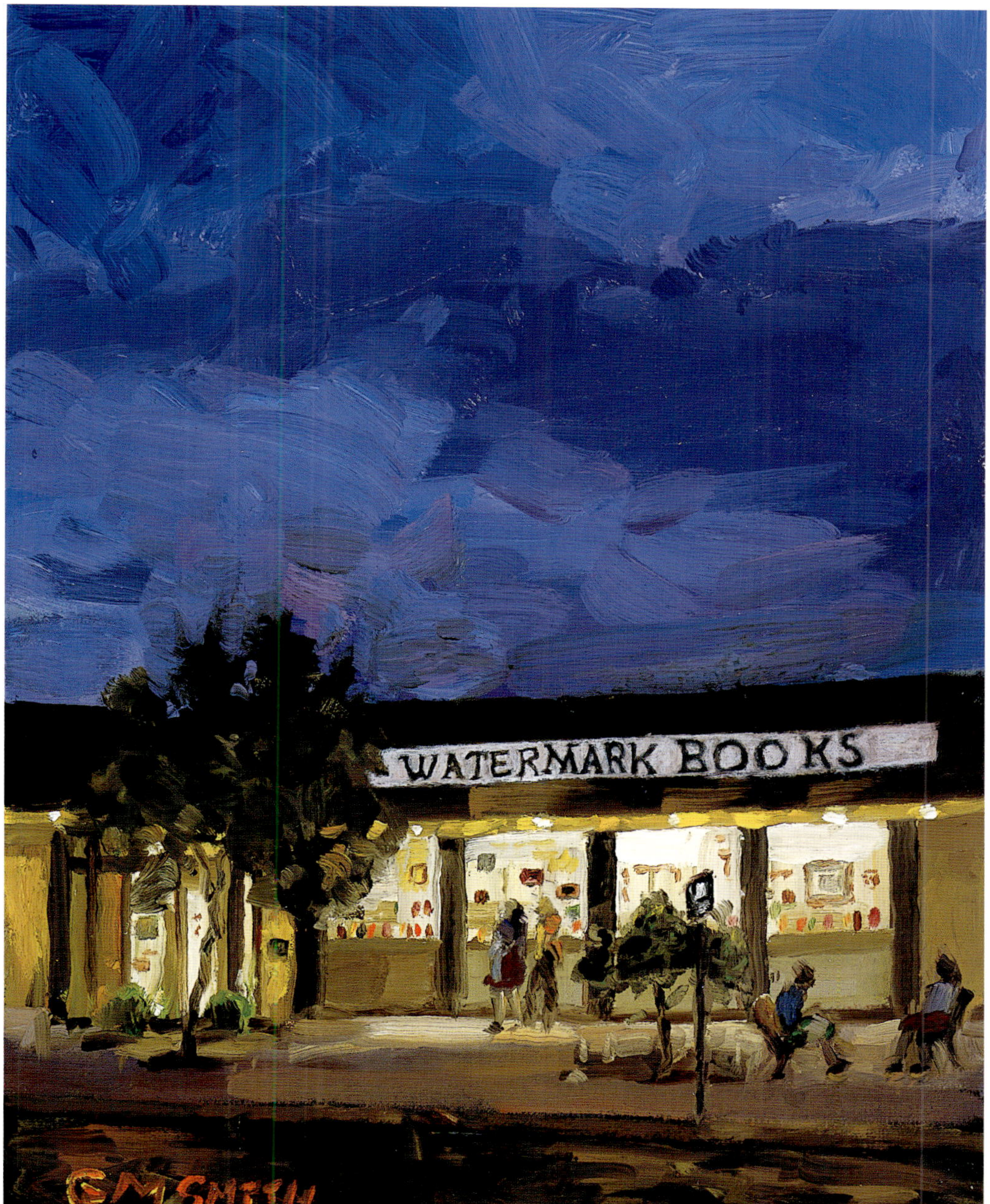

Gibbs M. Smith, Watermark Books, *2002. Oil on linen, 16" × 20".*

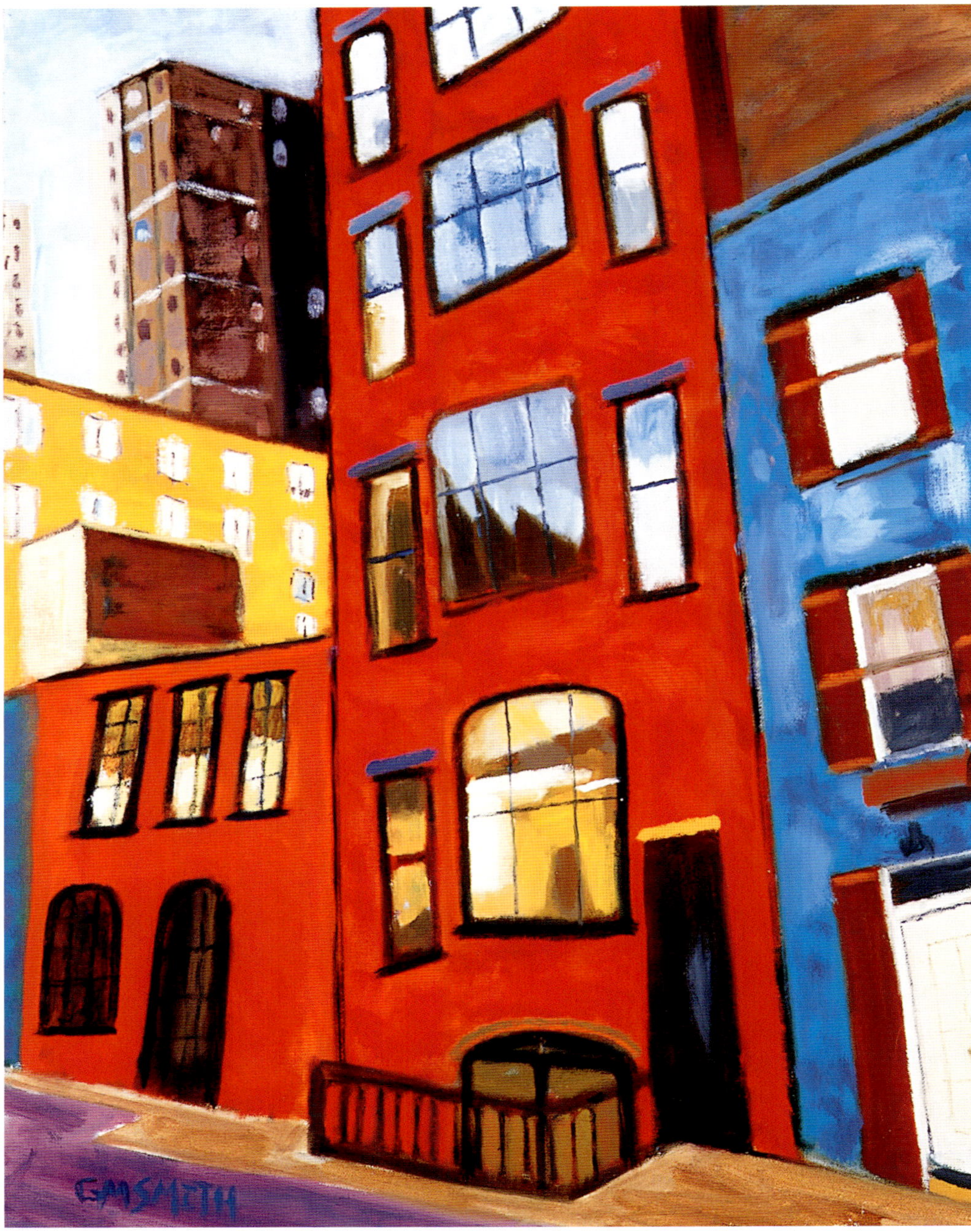

Gibbs M. Smith, Edward Hopper's Studio, *1985. Oil on linen, 16" × 20".*

Bookstores are one of the outward and visible signs of the inward truth of the central role of the book in the maintenance and augmentation of the culture. Absent the book, the fate of humankind would be that of still primitive savages. Only the presence of a continuing flow of thoughtful books into the hands of at least a significant fraction of the populace through the centuries staves off a kind of intellectual and ethical desert that would in time sap the very fruits of life leading to a sterile and near-meaningless existence.

So, salute the culture the book imparts and make use of the bookstores, which bring to the reader the enjoyment of the old and new fruits of culture.

—Richard Abel

You know you've read a good book when you turn the last page and feel a little as if you have lost a friend.

—Paul Sweeney

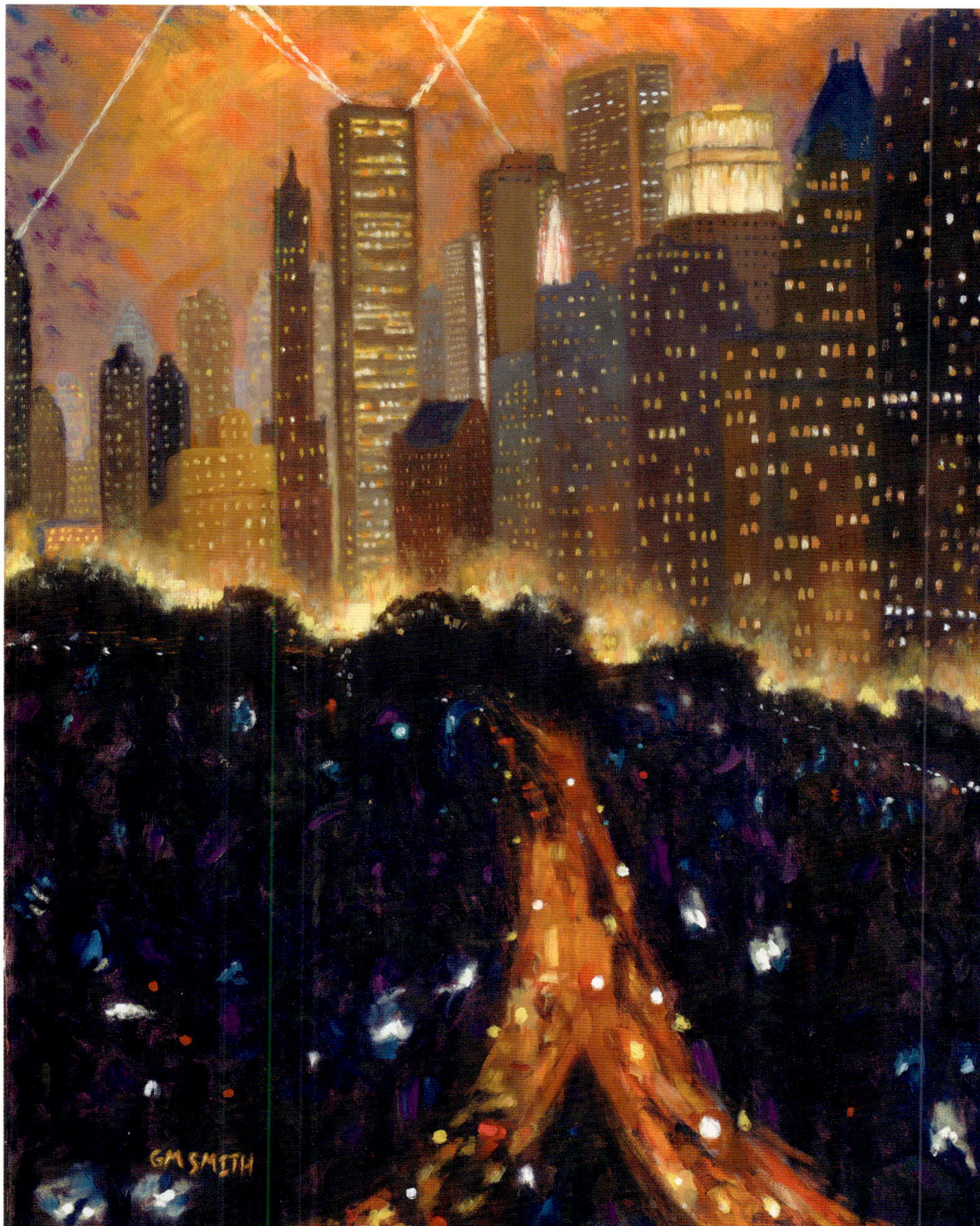

Gibbs M. Smith, Manhattan in the Rain, View from Central Park. *Oil on linen, 1991.*

Just the knowledge that a good book is awaiting one at the end of a long day makes the day happier.

—**Kathleen Norris**

Resources

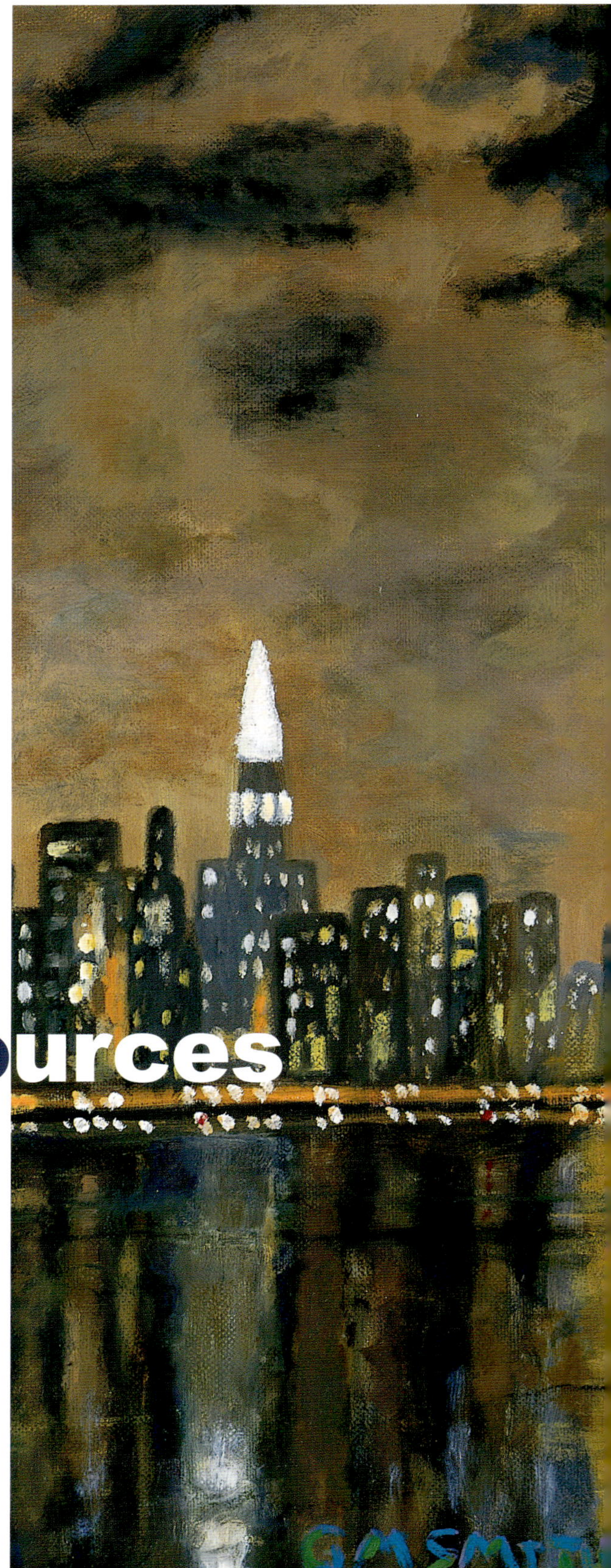

Gibbs M. Smith, Bridge, Manhattan, *1995. Oil on linen, 24" × 36".*

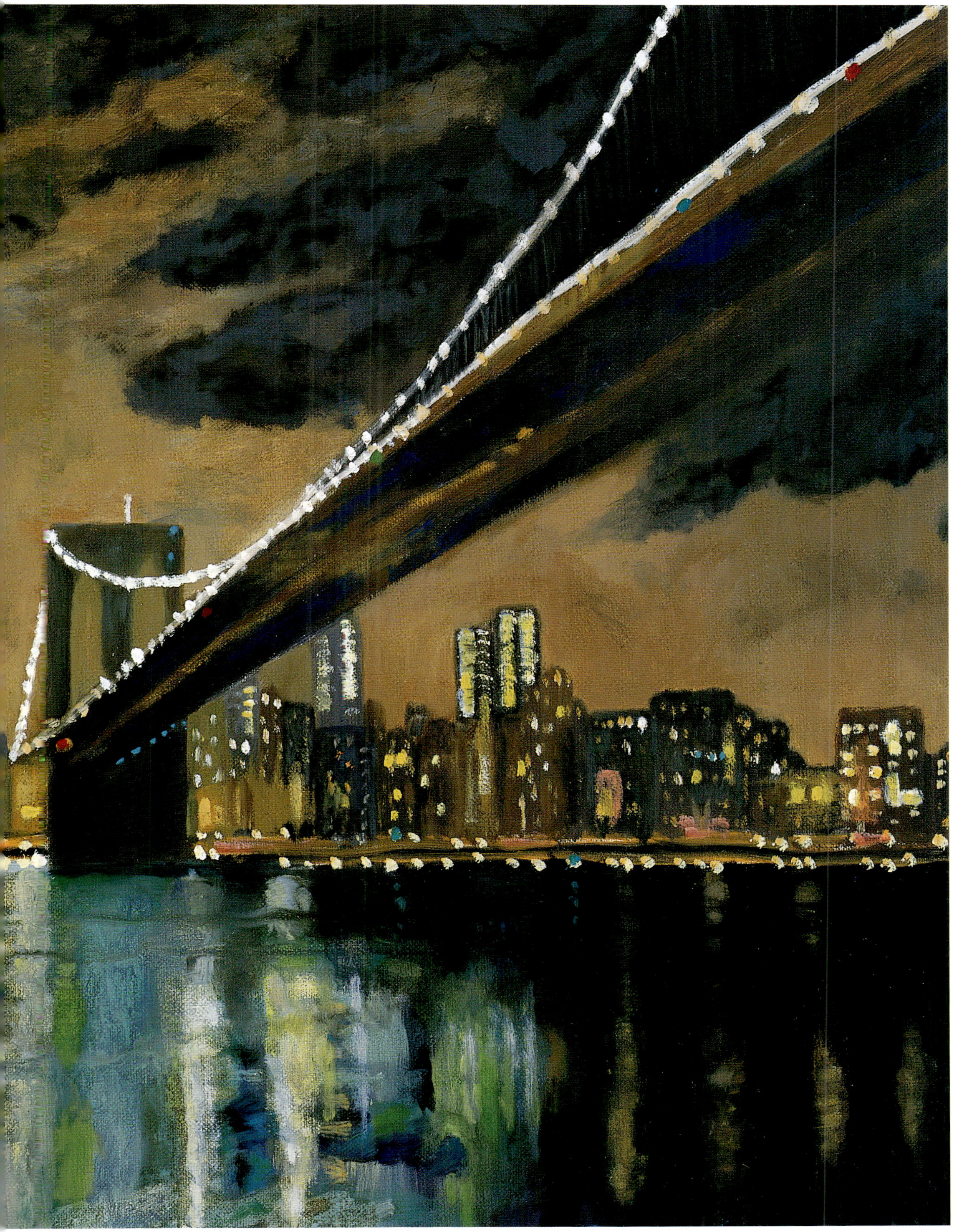

El Ateneo Grand Splendid
1860 Ave. Santa Fe
Buenos Aires, Argentina
54.11.4811.6104

Bank Street Bookstore
Broadway and 112th St.
New York, NY 10025
212.678.1654
bankstreetbooks.com

Barnes & Noble at Union Square
33 East 17th St.
New York, NY 10003
212.253.0810
barnesandnoble.com for more locations

Book Soup
8818 Sunset Blvd.
West Hollywood, CA 90069
310.659.3110
800.764.BOOK
booksoup.com

Borders
612 E. Liberty Street
Ann Arbor, MI 48104
734.668.7652
borders.com for more locations

Books & Books
265 Aragon Ave.
Coral Gables, FL 33134
305.442.4408
booksandbooks.com for more locations

Broadway Books
1714 NE Broadway
Portland, OR 97232
503.284.1726
broadwaybooks.net

Builders Booksource
1817 4th St.
Berkeley, CA 94710
800.843.2028
buildersbooksource.com for more locations

Changing Hands
6428 S. McClintock Dr.
Tempe, AZ 85283
480.730.0205
changinghands.com

Chapters: A Literary Bookstore
445 11th St. NW
Washington, D.C. 20004
202.737.5553
chaptersliterary.com

Chaucer's Books
3321 State St.
Santa Barbara, CA 93105
805.682.6787
chaucers.booksense.com

Christopher's Books
1400 18th St. (at Missouri)
San Francisco, CA 94107
415.255.8802
christophersbooks.com

City Lights Books
261 Columbus Ave. at
Broadway (North Beach)
San Francisco, CA 94133
415.362.8193
citylights.com

Collected Works
208 W. San Francisco St. #B
Santa Fe, NM 87501
877.988.4226
collectedworksbooks.com

The Corner Bookstore
1313 Madison Ave.
New York City, NY 10128
212.831.3554

The Cottage Book Shop
5989 Lake St.
Glen Arbor, MI 49636
231.334.4223
cottagebooks.com

The Depot Bookstore & Café
87 Throckmorton Ave.
Mill Valley, CA 94941
415.383.2665
depotbookstore.com

D.G. Wills Books
7461 Girard Ave.
La Jolla, CA 92037
858.456.1800
dgwillsbooks.com

Dutton's Beverly Hills Books
447 N. Canon Dr.
Beverly Hills, CA 90210
310.281.0997
duttonsbeverlyhills.com

The Elliott Bay Book Company
101 S. Main St.
Seattle, WA 98104
800.962.5311
elliottbaybook.com

Garcia Street Books
376 Garcia St.
Santa Fe, NM 87501
505.986.0151
garciastreetbooks.com

Green Apple Books
506 Clement St.
San Francisco, CA 94118
415.387.2272
greenapplebooks.com

Hennessey + Ingalls
214 Wilshire Blvd.
Santa Monica, CA 90401
310.458.9074
hennesseyingalls.com

Ken Sanders Rare Books
268 S. 200 E.
Salt Lake City, UT 84111
801.521.3819
kensanders.com

Kepler's Books
1010 El Camino Real
Menlo Park, CA 94025
650.324.4321
keplers.com

The King's English
1511 S. 1500 E.
Salt Lake City, UT 84105
801.484.9100
kingsenglish.com

Kramerbooks & Afterwords
1517 Connecticut Ave.
Washington, D.C. 20036
kramers.com

Maria's Bookshop
960 Main Ave.
Durango, CO 81301
970.247.1438
mariasbookshop.com

Mrs. Dalloway's Literary & Garden Arts
2904 College Ave.
Berkeley, CA 94705
510.704.8222
mrsdalloways.com

Page and Palette
32 South Section St.
Fairhope, AL 36532
251.928.5295
pageandpalette.com

Politics and Prose Bookstore
5015 Connecticut Ave., NW
Washington, D.C. 20008
202.364.1919
politics-prose.com

Powell's Books
1005 W. Burnside
Portland, OR 97209
800.878.7323
powells.com for more locations

Prairie Avenue Bookshop
418 South Wabash
Chicago, IL 60605
800.474.2724
pabook.com

Prairie Lights Books
15 S. Dubuque Street
Iowa City, IA 52240
319.337.2681
prairielightsbooks.com

Riverow Bookshop
87 Front St.
Owego, NY 13827
607.687.4094

Rizzoli Bookstore
31 West 57th St.
New York, NY 10019
800.52.BOOKS
212.759.2424
rizzoliusa.com

R.J. Julia Independent Booksellers
768 Boston Post Rd.
Madison, CT 06443
203.245.3959
800.74.READS
rjjulia.com

Sam Weller's Zion Bookstore
254 S. Main St.
Salt Lake City, UT 84101
801.328.2586
800.333.SAMW
samwellers.com

Shakespeare & Co. Bookstore
716 Broadway at Washington Place
New York, NY
212.529.1330
shakeandco.com for more locations

Shakespeare & Co.
37 rue de la Bûcherie
75005 Paris
00 33 (0) 1 43 25 40 93
shakespeareandcompany.com

Skylight Books
1818 N. Vermont Ave.
Los Angeles, CA 90027
323.660.1175
skylightbooks.com

St. Mark's Bookshop
31 Third Ave.
New York, NY 10003
212.260.7853
stmarksbookshop.com

Strand Book Store
828 Broadway (at 12th St.)
New York, NY 10003
212.473.1452
strandbooks.com

Tattered Cover Book Store
1628 16th St.
Denver, CO 80202
303.436.1070
tatteredcover.com for more locations

Tecolote Book Shop
1470 E. Valley Rd.
Santa Barbara, CA 93108
805.969.4977

That Bookstore in Blytheville
316 W. Main
Blytheville, AR 72315
870.763.3333
tbib.com

Three Lives & Company
154 West 10 St.
New York, NY 10014
212.741.2069
threelives.com

Village Books
1200 Eleventh St.
Bellingham, WA 98225
360.671.2626
villagebooks.com

Vroman's Bookstore
695 E. Colorado Blvd.
Pasadena, CA 91101
626.449.5320
vromansbookstore.com

Warwick's
7812 Girard Ave.
La Jolla, CA 92037
858.454.0347
warwicks.com

Watermark Books & Café
4701 East Douglas
Wichita, KS 67218
316.682.1181

Good as it is to inherit a library,
it is better to collect one.

—Augustine Birrell,
Obiter Dicta

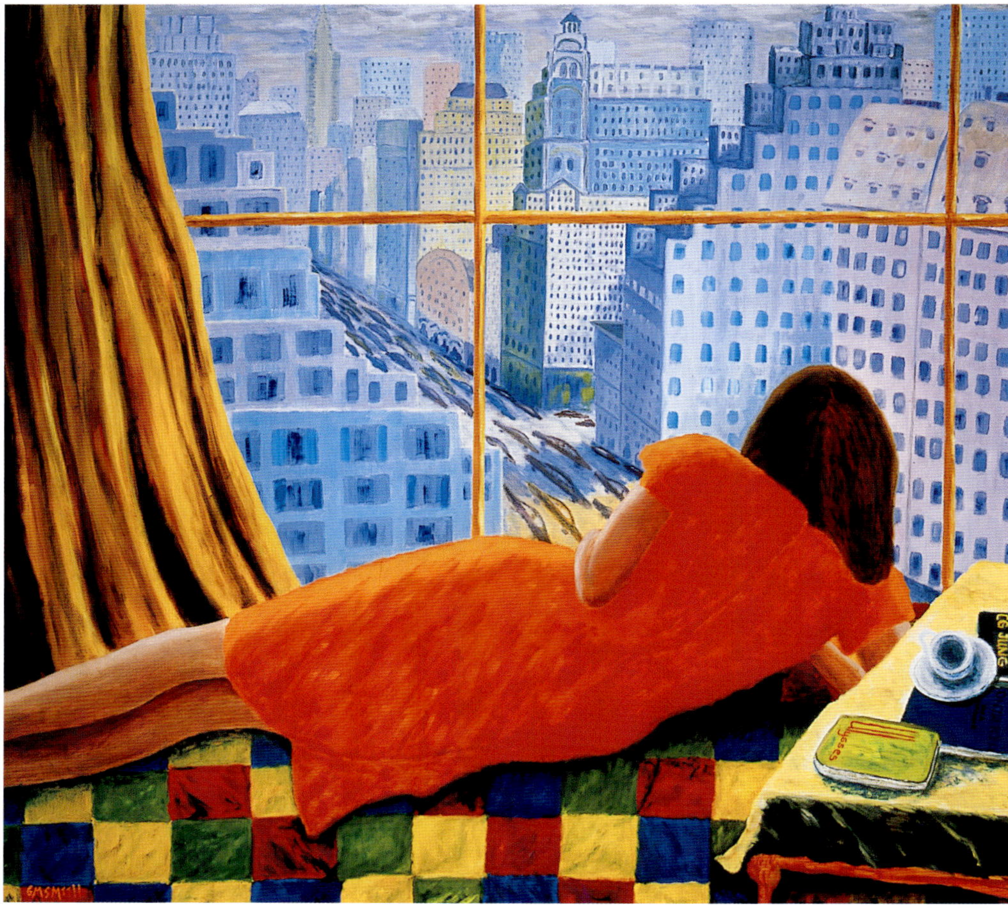

Gibbs M. Smith, Dreaming and Reading in the City. *Oil on linen, 16″ × 20″.*

People need to understand that they can lose their stress, fears, and anxieties in the written word, learn new coping mechanisms in someone else's struggles, travel to calm places without leaving their home. Books make us greater than we are.

—Midge Dey

tand Bookwork Bookends Bookrack Bookwork Bookman Booklist Bookstall Bookreader Bookmak

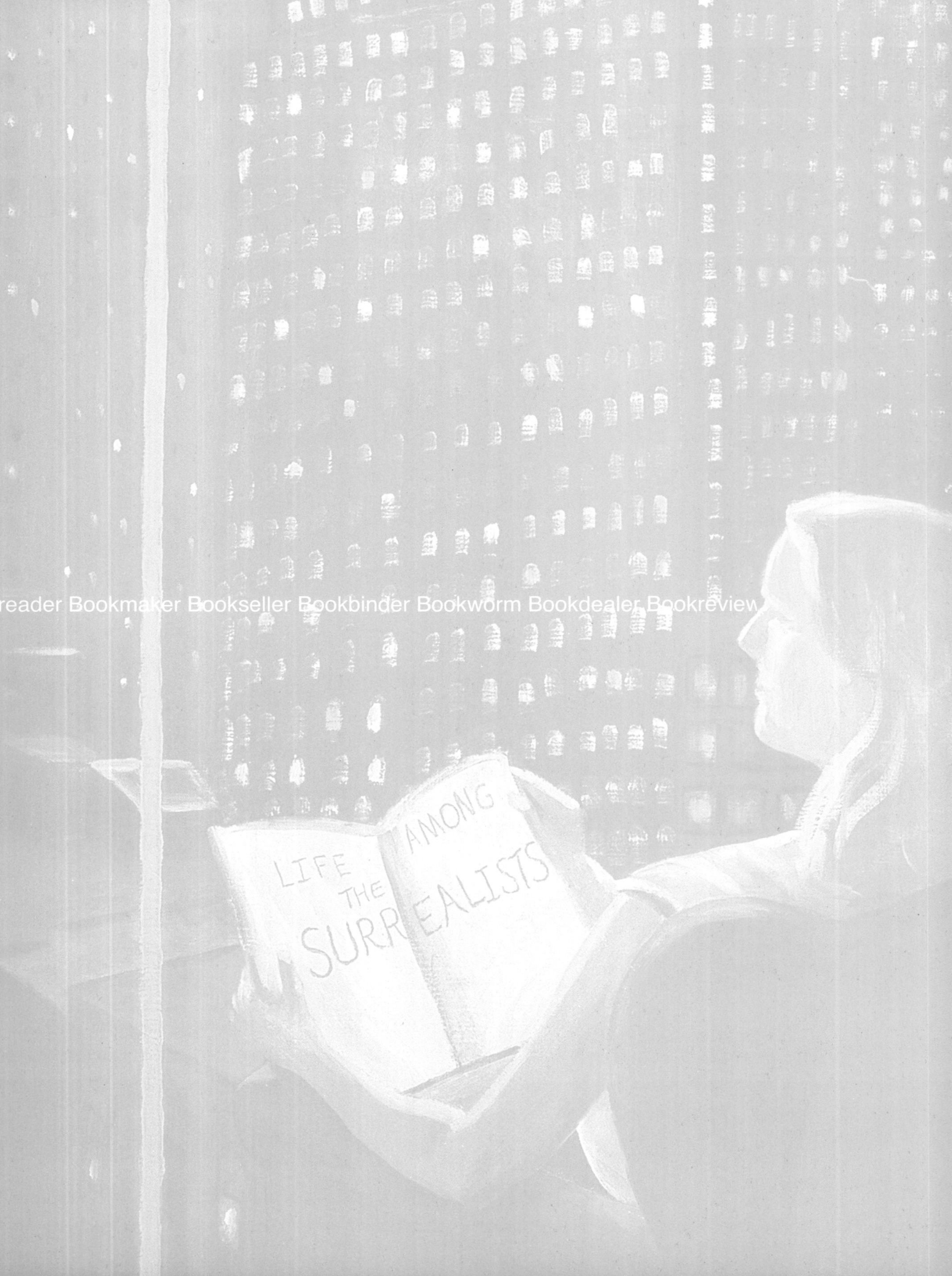
reader Bookmaker Bookseller Bookbinder Bookworm Bookdealer Bookreview
LIFE AMONG THE SURREALISTS